FIVE FAREWELLS

A SOUTHERN LIFE WITH DISSOCIATIVE IDENTITY DISORDER

BY

LIZ ELLIOT

Printed in the United States of America
Published by WingSpan Press, Livermore, CA
www.wingspanpress.com
The WingSpan name, logo and colophon are the
trademarks of WingSpan Publishing.

First Edition 2010
ISBN 978-1-59594-380-4
Library of Congress Control Number: 2010925069

This Memoir was written for Sherry.

I don't really know what to say exactly about what it meant for me that you came into my life. Some things seem too intimate to talk about. I do know to say that you got in the seat with me in my journey. You wouldn't allow me to be afraid of anything as you navigated our way. You always covered me. How do you put that into words that anyone would understand except for you and me? I can't forget you. I will always love you. You are a part of my eternal family. No day will ever go by that I won't think of you. No day will ever go by that I won't stop and remember how you looked at our lives.

Special thanks to Photographer, Edward Babcock.

What I am with you is the Self that I want to be forever, somewhere in the middle of light and dark, I think. You teach me what it means to live in the essence of myself. Congratulations, my dear friend, on living your highest truth, and Congratulations for living that truth, with the highest, most beautiful love of your spiritual life.

Special thanks also to Mary Cook, for modeling for me the greatest compassion of soul. Knowing you has made what I will be in my journey very clear. I came to you with my bag strapped over my shoulder, and I left with empty hands, feeling weightless, knowing for the first time that I would be free.

TABLE OF CONTENTS

PROLOGUE 1

    Chapter 1   Jess Was a Giant 3
    Chapter 2   My Mother's Funeral 5
    Chapter 3   Learning to Drown 9
    Chapter 4   Leslie Holds My Memories 13

EARLY CHILDHOOD 17

    Chapter 1   The Boy Next Door 18
    Chapter 2   Mother Was a Mystery 21
    Chapter 3   The Partial Screendoor 25
    Chapter 4   Gretchen 28
    Chapter 5   The Hospital 32
    Chapter 6   Aunt May 35
    Chapter 7   Church 38
    Chapter 8   Kindergarten 42
    Chapter 9   Two Teachers 45
    Chapter 10 Darrell 49
    Chapter 11 Food 52

MY FOUR BROTHERS 55

    Chapter 1   Jessie 56
    Chapter 2   The Jessie-Elizabeth 60
    Chapter 3   The Woods 62
    Chapter 4   The Dream 67
    Chapter 5   Quentin 70
    Chapter 6   Brent 72
    Chapter 7   Keith 76

THE MOTHER 79

    Chapter 1   The Mother 80
    Chapter 2   The Floating Grandmother 82
    Chapter 3   Home 85
    Chapter 4   The Cupcakes 89

Chapter 5   Karo Syrup 94
Chapter 6   Christmas 97

AL **103**

Chapter 1   Meeting Al 104
Chapter 2   The Red Water Pump 108
Chapter 3   Night Time 112
Chapter 4   Away From Home 115
Chapter 5   Another World 120
Chapter 6   My Father's Visit 122
Chapter 7   Sunnie 125
Chapter 8   Little House on the Prairie 129
Chapter 9   Mother Finds Out 132
Chapter 10 Stung By Bees 137
Chapter 11 Asking About Al 141

ON THE RIVER **145**

Chapter 1   The Gods of Water 146
Chapter 2   Claire 149
Chapter 3   The River Community 152
Chapter 4   Gone With the Wind 156
Chapter 5   Back Home With Mother 162

DOWN SOUTH **165**

Chapter 1   Going Down South 166
Chapter 2   High on the Mountain of Love 170
Chapter 3   Rhett 174
Chapter 4   Kay 179

FOUR FAREWELLS **183**

Chapter 1   Kay's Death 184
Chapter 2   Kay's Funeral 188
Chapter 3   Paul 193
Chapter 4   Leslie 197
Chapter 5   Goodbye, Mother 200

LIVING IN THE PRESENT **205**

    Chapter 1   Imagine.. 206
    Chapter 2   Starting to Heal 209
    Chapter 3   The Seasonal Soul.................................. 215
    Chapter 4   Telling Mother About My Multiplicity ... 219
    Chapter 5   Breaking the Cycle................................. 222

GOING HOME AGAIN **225**

Afterword 230

PROLOGUE

1

JESS WAS A GIANT

Jess was a giant! It wasn't because I was so small; he was just big all over. I looked at him when he was a man. He stood maybe six foot four. This was after I had not known him since we were children. I stood face to face with my beautiful Indian brother, his facial features sharp, his strides high and heavy. I couldn't get over how invisible I had felt in childhood, and how once again I would feel completely invisible looking up just to say a simple hello. It was humbling! I'd go away and leave my family, and come back still being nothing of significance. I was the odd one out.

Leslie would say, "Go write your story, go tell the world the truth if it makes you feel any better. Just get over it! You could come back," she would say. "I'll always love you . . . ," she would say. "I'll always forgive you." The words rang out, drilling in my head for years.

But … she would not forgive me, and I didn't ever write the story. I wrote a world inside of myself, but Leslie did not love me for it, she did not forgive me for it, and she did not ever welcome me home again. She was lovely, Leslie was lovely, and nothing about her soul was heavy. She had been adopted.

I won't go methodically through each of my siblings. One I avoided because he hurt me. I don't think he, Brent, meant to hurt me. I think he was ill. We were all ill back then. Another of my siblings, Quentin, wanted to be our father and he studied that notion until there was no one left to possibly father. My brother, Keith, was kind; he loved his children, and never bothered anyone. He found solace in watching his children live real lives. It was amazing to him that every time he looked at his children they were living a happy life like he'd seen on TV. He never minded my heavy heart or my heavy presence.

Leslie asked me once, "Why write? Why not choose a life to bury yourself in? Why not live like everyone else?" Her exasperation was harsh and clear.

I stammered that I did not know, and tried to explain that I had lost time in early childhood, blackouts, that skewed my perceptions. I swore to her that I did not know why I could not live.

Leslie wailed out in frustration, "What's that about? Be glad you don't remember. That's life; it's the way that it is. I hate it that you're like this." She didn't notice that I hung my head in the deepest and most incredible shame.

"You don't have a job, you drift, you don't do anything! Let it go, for God's sake. Forget who you were, reinvent, do what I do. Fake your way through. Your weight drags us all down and it wouldn't matter if you were on another planet, we would all still feel it!" She cut me into a million pieces.

"You're selfish, Lizzy, you're selfish and it's unbearable." She finally just turned her elegant little face away. She was a blonde waif; her eyes reminded me of the sea. Not a truly clever description I guess, but they did remind me of the sea. They reminded me of the sea when you can't tell if it's blue or green in all the mix of flashing whitecaps. I was midnight, and she was life.

"Yes, you must be right," I stammered.

What I really wanted to tell my sister was that I write because I'm afraid that I will disappear if I don't sketch everything down. I'm afraid of losing time and not knowing who or what I was before. The truth is that I need proof that I lived in that time that I shared with her. In essence, I was also afraid of becoming her, some unclear and fearful identity.

I wanted to convey to my sister that I wrote because I didn't want *any* of us to disappear. It wasn't just me I was scared for. In my screwed up way I was somehow living with the fear that we had never been real and we'd never existed.

I've had this constant need to prove to myself that we as a whole were not a myth, and that we had in fact lived a life together. I ached with all of this, and there was no way to tell her that. I was complex and my sister didn't do complex. She never did.

2

MY MOTHER'S FUNERAL

His hands were broad and mighty wrapped around her grey marble urn. Grief stung his features along with the rainy hard cold in the air. I'd imagined the day they laid my mother to rest being cold and brisk, not rainy, not absorbent . . . not tolerant of her life . . . not painful for me.

I'd imagined in my past a movie scene where we all looked superior to what we ever looked like in our ordinary lives. The sun would be high in my mind. The cold would comfort me. Mother Earth herself would whisper in my ear that it all had come to a peaceful and dignified end. It didn't, though, come to that dignified quiet end, and though I waited for her death to free me, I did not find freedom in it.

Instead, Jess held her urn in his massive hands on the rainiest... coldest...November day. We watched and clutched ourselves, bitterly and utterly broken.

They laid my mother, Susan, to rest in the wind on the same river bank where my grandmother, her mother, had brought her as a nine year old child to force her to sleep with my grandmother's current bored lover. My mother on the river bank fought her way free of the man in question by taking her coke bottle opener from her back pocket and bringing it up his back. My grandmother was angry with her nuisance of a daughter, but from my understanding she was not really articulate enough to give the situation much energy beyond sudden annoyance.

I don't know that my grandmother wasn't smart. It was always my perception that she was just tired and trying to survive. She had eight children with no husband, and no money. I believe she washed other people's clothes to help feed her children. My grandfather worked on the trains, and was always gone, and they were divorced in the latter part of their lives after all of the children were born, or actually I think maybe the next to the last one was conceived after the divorce.

You can see that I don't know much about my grandmother. I don't even know her name. My mother would not share it. My grandmother died before I was born. I look at old pictures of her. I see my mother and myself in her eyes. I wonder about her. I wonder about the things she did to my mother. It's the kind of thing that would make Leslie go out of her mind.

"Don't ask her any questions! You're pissing me off! Leave her alone, or I swear to you I'll walk out of here and leave you with her." Leslie's anger left its imprint on my life. She was our mother's late life caregiver.

"She acted like she wanted to talk. She was asking me questions. What did you want me to do?" I was in my early twenties. This was before I'd left my family for good.

"You're so fucking inconsiderate! Everything's about you!" She threw herself in a chair and all chairs were too big for her. She drew her knees up tight, grabbed the remote control and smoked obsessively.

Mama had Leslie in the most peculiar way emotionally. Leslie felt a loyalty to her because she adopted her when she was eleven years old.

In my early twenties I found Mother outside in the dark on her back porch going out of her mind. Leslie had gone out somewhere, and asked that I come by to check on her.

"Mama, what's wrong? It's cold, let's go inside." Her gown was bright blue, and silky. She always wore this kind of gown.

"She sent him to my room." Her hands were wringing.

"Mama, let's go inside." I reached for the screen door.

"I'm not going inside. You need to know this." She wouldn't look me in the eyes. She never did when she was vulnerable.

"We can't talk until we get you inside. I just want to get you out of the cold." Her back porch unnerved me. I hated even being in the yard I grew up in. All of it frightened me.

"She sent him to my room, Lizzy."

"Who? Who did she send to your room? Who's she?"

"Him."

6

She stared into the night at nothing.

"Him who?" I shouted. The wind moved so loudly around us that I had to shout.

"My Father!" She seemed to be getting something that I wasn't getting.

"Grandpa went into your room, okay. Why, why did she send him? Who sent him?" As the words left my lips, my legs went wobbly, my chest tightened. I wanted to disappear.

"My mother sent your grandfather to my room. She didn't want to be with him. I heard her tell him that she didn't want him and to just go get what he wanted from Susan."

Her voice fell into the wind. Her hands stopped wringing. She seemed to be peaceful again.

I fell into the empty seat across the table from her. I hung my head in my hands and did not feel the cold. I didn't want to know anything about what happened to my mother at that time. I was sincerely struggling with my own life, but my mother would never have considered my feelings on that.

I eased my head up, "I'm sorry, Mama, I'm sorry. I'm so sorry for all that she did to you."

She didn't say any more about it. She solidly grabbed her cigarettes and went inside. I held the door for her as I saw her getting up. I watched her pick up a book off the kitchen counter and make her way down the hall. I heard as she clicked the lock, returned to her cave, and started her old steel fan running.

I will not give my mother the pardon she wanted even with her being dead. I do not forgive her, even with her pain. She was not feeble. I do not accept that. She was a force, and in choosing to live, she did not choose us. She was powerful. She taught me to be a woman, though it was the wrong kind of woman. She was a capable person. She was not the world she tried to hide in when she would finally go low.

So, Jess holds the urn, as our hearts go bleak.

Leslie stood on a grassy hill in the distance. Black was never her color. It just made her look anorexic. Jess was in dramatic black as well. The suit fit his character. It matched that dark native hair. He was a work of art, a masculine structure to behold. His cheeks were pale and tear streaked. When did he get so fucking soft?

My heart screamed in silence. Quentin just seethed in my direction. Just come over and hit me, I thought; that's what you want to do anyway. Just hit me, strike me down. Maybe that will lessen your pain somehow. Maybe I'll feel something.

Keith came in jeans and a nice shirt. How he loved our mother! Why in the world that was, I do not know. She worshiped Jess and Quentin and didn't give a damn about Keith or Brent. They shared a father she did not like.

Brent, by the way, could not be found for the occasion. They were not completely sure if he was alive due to his severe drug and alcohol problems. Somehow my siblings forgive him, though. He didn't talk about our lives. He just tried to forget everything on a daily basis. Somehow that was more noble than my existence.

As for my grandmother, may God look at her the way He wishes and the way that He will. She was a quiet woman who worked hard to raise her children alone. She was a monster in the nightmares of a daughter who didn't stand a chance to be anything whole or right. When my mother was barely grown and into a bad early marriage, my grandmother took the two babies of the five left at home and left the oldest three children on the steps of a children's home to become wards of the state. Her new lover did not think he could handle so many children.

My mother fought to get and raise her siblings who were left on the steps; at least that's the way she told it. The kids ended up in homes, though. She did not understand how her mother could do that to her own children, and she did not do it to us, her children. She reminded us often of how she did not abandon us. I'm sure we all wished that she had.

Jess's wrist flexed with the urn's swing. The trees swayed in the cold rainy wind. The river ran quietly and didn't seem to mind our presence, as I'm betting it didn't sixty-eight years ago, when my mother struggled free with a coke bottle opener.

My fists clenched involuntarily as the gray rain of ash started to rise.

Mama didn't want a funeral. She did not live a good life. She did not want the whispers and the falseness of people gathered around her dead body. I don't blame her in the least.

8

3

LEARNING TO DROWN

My purpose now is to tell the truth, the whole truth. For many years I knew nothing about the truth. All I had were mixed reactions to the colors in the sky, to the smell of something that turned me on my heels, or the cold weather which seemed to bring more peace to me than the heat of summer.

I saw life as an illusion. I seemed to perceive things, instances, in odd separate dimensional forms. I remember holding a small hand into the light of the sun and just being filled with wonder at my own translucence. That wonder still resides in me. I'm still reacting; I'm still fascinated by the glory of simply living. I'm not an enemy to life. I'm not bitter. I think it's all quite perfect really.

The sun was so bright on the river. It was bright, but we didn't feel the full force of it through the overhanging trees. It was the golden rays that gleamed through the trees that has me mentioning it. The memory is soothing somehow.

My mother and father owned a cabin on a river which I will not geographically place. The cabin was just a short way from the river bank, and for this it flooded some in the rainy seasons.

When I place myself on the river bank, I see a variety of things. I see the way the cabin was old, rustic, and almost dilapidated. I see the docks that led down to the murky, mystical, brown flowing waters. There were two docks.

I also see the way we could only catch glimpses of our piece of the river because trees were grown all around the narrow part we lived on. The only opening for a ways down was the opening to our isolated wooded cabin.

But, let me tell you what I hear in my mind while I'm watching. I

9

hear Leslie squealing with delight. I hear Keith playing some nameless game of water tag with Jess and Brent. I hear Quentin telling to whoever would listen that he bet that he could race and beat all three of them to the other side and back. I hear my father's wonderful voice shout some innocent direction to one of us while he is working on his boat. Mostly, though, I hear the workings of children's clear and pure laughter. The splashing thrills me as I sit aside at maybe three years old because I could not swim.

I watched them, my siblings. I was afraid of the water. I could not swim until I was around nine years old. They would have to put me on a safe part of the river bank wall where I could hold on, to enjoy the water. It was a nuisance for my family. The kids needed to swim; we spent most of our lives on a river, on an ocean. Our worlds were surrounded by one water form or another.

I'd heard my parents' motto in teaching kids to swim was to just throw them in and watch for a while to see if they resurfaced. I know for a fact that's how Jess learned to swim. In truth, it's the way I learned to not swim until I was nine, but it's not for the reasons that you think.

My family didn't know about my fantasy worlds or anything about my translucent feelings of only slight existence. I didn't feel that attached to my body, or physical life. When it was my turn to be thrown into the water, they were taken aback by what happened with me.

How could they have known that I would not struggle? How were they to know that they would have to dive to find me? How were they to know that I would simply wrap my mind around the stunning, vivid, light brown bubbles? How could they know that the water was such a peaceful escape for me?

My father threw me at three into the river out to my brother Keith who was waiting close to the other side. It happened just like that. He grabbed one of my legs and one of my arms and flung me. My body went limp and my mind went away. I remember this odd tune-out or dismissal of the moment that surged through me. I didn't feel any pain, and I remember precisely my feelings as I slid deeper down into the restful waters.

I wasn't suffering as I sank. I didn't feel any lung collapsing that I'd heard happens when you're under the water too long. I watched the bubbles closely and knew they were coming from the breath leaving my body. I never once grabbed for the surface. It didn't occur to me. The bubbles were rising into the sun, that light place that was slowly becoming darker as I sank. Why in the world would the bubbles want to go there?

My father treated me differently after that, in what slight nuances I can recall. He watched me more closely, with worry, like he was unsure about the things I might do. I guess looking back, I could tell that he saw me as unwell, but he was not okay with saying it.

I don't know who found me and brought me back to the surface. No tears came as my father laid me out on the dock, choking out water. I didn't grab for him the way I suppose a normal human would. I just lay there blankly. The dock was warm, my sensations were heightened.

"Lizzy, are you okay, are you okay?" His voice was panicked. His realizing the stupidity of what he'd just done was alive in his tone. I sputtered water; he helped me to my side enough to release the water when it came up.

He tried talking to me again, but I couldn't speak to answer. "Lizzy, Lizzy, are you okay?" He was louder and had started rattling my arm and tapping hard at my face.

I finally acknowledged with my dead blank nod as he reached up to clasp both of his hands to his tired, worn face. He was at his knees over me.

I often wonder, in my adult life, when my father is drinking, as he does often . . . is he still there . . . at his knees, over me? Does he reach a point in his drinking where he realizes he's gone too far, "I should've passed on that last Scotch," because his head goes back to that moment with me on the dock? It might seem funny to anyone that I would wonder, but my own head when in duress certainly goes back to that moment. It was key for me. I felt I lost my father in a whole different way in that particular time.

I lay there, looking in an empty fashion into my father's eyes. I couldn't speak, but I also couldn't respond with any reaction he could understand. Children react to fear. I never did. I lay and looked up at him, like, what's next, what do you want? Are you throwing me in again? What's next? Tell me how to respond. I didn't mean to be out of my head at three. I didn't mean to not have normal responses to pain.

Later in life I would learn to react to pain like other people do, but generally it's for everyone else to feel better, it's not for me. I think I feel bad for Paul, my father, now. No one wants the truth of what their children are put into their faces that darkly. Did he wonder what in the world he and my mother had done to me to make me the way that I was? He must have, or . . . maybe he knew.

When I was small, he called me his little Lizzy Brat with pure affection. He loved to pull my wispy light brown hair out of my face where it would be stuck to my fat sticky little cheeks. He bought me grape soda long after I'd stopped drinking it. He had no words, and he held my hand. He watched me and my difficulties with existence as long as he was able. This goes to show you, that in life everything is perfect, really, even the bad. All, good and bad, has its way of showing our humanity on high, and how are we otherwise to see it?

My father made mistakes, but we existed in our time. I was his little Lizzy, and God bless, because he loved me. So what if he valued his own life above ours in the end? Who knows what was going on in his head? He still lives on the river. I've always held a fondness for him.

In staying to the truth, I can share that these days on the river are the last days that I knew them, my family. I do not remember my mother on the river. I don't have a single memory of her before my father left our family. It's like she didn't arrive in the scene until way late.

My family taught me fiction; they taught me the hard beauty of truth. Mostly they taught me to spend my life remembering and deciphering which was which. I want to say up front now how I loved each of them. I think that telling the truth now will be the only way I could ever truly let them know that. It is so that they will be done with me. I'll have to live with that.

4

LESLIE HOLDS MY MEMORIES

L eslie holds my memories from the age of two until the age of five. My siblings would all have different roles to play with each other in our lives together. Sadly, I believe my role with Leslie was to be the face that kept this life real, up front, and the truths of it unavoidable. I'm sorry to have been the one with that job. It made our relationship the one that didn't work. It had no peace in it.

She spent our lives loving me, and shoving me away. I can't tell you the countless times she's stood beside me and when someone would ask how it happened that one of us was blonde and one of us was brunette, she would quickly announce to the world that she was adopted, and that not a part of the blood that coursed through my veins was hers. It was her ultimate jab. She felt it was safe, and would hurt me least. She was wrong.

Leslie wasn't always the way she is now. She and I had a very different relationship when we were young. Leslie is eleven years older than I am. She was the same age as Quentin. Keith was two years younger than Quentin. Brent was a year and a half younger than Keith, and Jess, the one that holds my heart differently, was only three years older than me.

Leslie came with her father, Paul, to a family of four boys, and my understanding is that this was terrifying for her. She carried a fragile body, and an extraordinarily luminous face. I have pictures of her then. She smiles the way my nieces do now, except my nieces don't have such an uncertainty hidden behind their eyes. Also, because Leslie was so thin, her eyes were ridiculously large.

She had a birthmark splashed across one arm; it was a deep chocolate color. My father used to ask me when I was small, "Who spilt coffee on your sister?" He would wait for me to laugh and I always would.

My beautiful sister loved a certain purple turtle. I wonder whatever happened to that turtle. Maybe Mother got rid of it. She had a way of coming in with a bag, with her children in a panic, and deciding what they didn't need any more. Just the smallest thing I will blame her for, but how many parents finally do that?

When Paul married Susan, he had Leslie, and she, Susan, had the boys. I came into the group just after they were all united as a family. I was Susan's sister Kay's daughter. At sixteen months old I was adopted by my aunt Susan because my mother could not take care of me.

Leslie took refuge in me, but she also took refuge in Jess. I think that she must have made it her responsibility to take care of us, the youngest. It makes sense that she would create responsibility for herself to create some kind of order for herself at the same time. I could not say that she was asked to care for us, the youngest two. We were not cared for or watched over by our parents in that way. We were six kids that were seen and not heard. The idea was that we had all better be glad that we had a roof over our head, and food to eat. That was the extent of their parenting.

When my father left us when I was four, the leaving spun our worlds out of control, out of reason really. He forced Leslie away screaming at fifteen years old. Leslie didn't want to go with her dad; she wanted to stay with our mother. I have to wonder why anyone would have chosen our mother over our father.

Leslie is my memory keeper, if only in those three years before she left with our father. She comes to me in dreams as a fifteen year old girl. I'm four years old. The dreams are like movie pictures on an old reel that you play on the wall at home.

In my dreams, Leslie isn't happy. She's nervous, skinny but tawny, with wide eyes, and doesn't know why she's alive at all. At fifteen, late at night on the reel, she's pushing open the screened back door that overlooks a deck that wasn't there at that juncture in time.

She's wearing the same blue sleeveless tee that was her favorite when we were young. The door creaks. I hear her call, "Lizzy, Lizzy, are you out here?" I can hear the chilling fear in her voice. Why does she want me? I want to know that when I have this dream. Why is she looking for me? Why is she so afraid?

Meanwhile, she doesn't notice me, but I'm under the deck, huddled and trembling, my knees drawn up in my very slightly pudgy four year old arms. I tremble and it isn't cold. Why am I hiding from Leslie?

Why in our adult lives won't she just tell me what happened, what memory I've lost?

I see her clearly; the scene is at some points panoramic. The movie goes to her and her voice, and then to me huddled under the deck, and then the panorama of the full scene.

I'm dirty. I have no direct feelings, but know that under the deck is where I'm staying. I feel the cool sand beneath my bottom in flowered panties. My head rests on a splintery supporting beam as I listen to her. My thin shoulder-length hair clings to my face a little, from sweat maybe. I'm numb, but trembling from the animal instinct to survive.

EARLY CHILDHOOD

1

THE BOY NEXT DOOR

When he asked me to go under the house, I just did it. I didn't know there was a choice to be made. Under the house he hung orange and brown cowboy sheets up to form a fort. The house was more off the ground than most houses. As children we would go and hide under that house, the house next door to mine.

The fort was a square shape large enough for three children to sit comfortably, but being three and small, maybe I just felt that it seemed large enough for three children.

I don't know where Leslie was at the time. I don't know where my father was. I don't know why I was asked to go under the house next door. Children ran wild in the country. No one noticed when we were gone unless we didn't come back.

What did he do? I could not tell you. All I have are the dreams and the walks over the property when I was young where I avoided the shreds of cowboy sheets still left hanging under the house.

"Lizzy, come here." His face was so round and chubby that it squinted his blank green eyes almost shut.

"Okay," I called back. It was a terribly hot day, and my hair was matted, dirty and wet from play. I'd been running around with Jess that afternoon playing Cowboys and Indians before he got bored of me. I always had to be the Indian.

"Look under here. I've made a house. I know a game we can play. Do you want to play?"

He was pointing under the house. His twelve year old voice seemed playful and excited. His striped red and green shirt was rising off his chubby tummy. He had on tan pants in the heat.

"Yes, I do," I called forward as I arrived where he was. I was looking at him with my hand shielding my eyes from the sun. The trees seemed like giants above my head. My knobby knees and bare feet were colored with dried brown mud. My soft white shorts flopped on my thighs. They were dirty too.

I don't know why I went under the house. I just always did what I was asked or told to do. Nobody was around to notice us. I don't know why we were alone. It seemed like there were always people around otherwise.

The boy, William, lived in the house next door with my mother's best friend Carol. The two women, Carol and my mother, grew up together. My Aunt Carol, as I called her, was married to a man at this time who had two boys. One boy was nice, and the other was not.

Aunt Carol got married when Mother got married. Aunt Carol got divorced when Mother got divorced. Aunt Carol got a new car when Mother got a new car. My Aunt Carol, who was very kind, had always been obsessed with Mother. They were together every day. They had a gate between their yards.

Mother married Paul who had a daughter. Aunt Carol married Mr. Gill who had two boys. We did, in our adult lives, speculate about our Aunt Carol's attachment to our mother. Aunt Carol was probably in love with Mother at some point, but those lives could not be lived in our environment, in that time, besides the fact that Mother certainly killed Aunt Carol's love for her by the end of their lives. Mother had a way of doing that.

I was on my knees following William into the cowboy fort. . . that's all I remember. I promise. My mind then goes black and that's the end, but my dreams tell me something different.

In the main recurring dream that I have, the wind blows hard, the thunder wells, and I'm running over to the house next door to get something for my mother. I'm a woman in this dream. I trip in the dream, and I feel as if I'm flying through the air. The wind throws me to the edge of the house where I first crawled under with William.

I see the curtain torn down and my little girl head sticking out from a hole that was dug the length of my body. It wasn't quite long enough for my whole body to lie completely flat. He's on his knees over me. I'm flat on my back. My body is naked. William is fully clothed. I don't know what he is doing, and I can't remember for anything.

The house next door has haunted my entire life. At one point I thought that I needed to go back there, peek under the house, and make sure I wasn't still there under the house. In telling the truth, I will admit, that I'm always in conflict about it.

Is there a part of me there still? Is little Lizzy waiting for me to come there? I don't know that I'll ever be brave enough to truly know.

2

MOTHER WAS A MYSTERY

I remember the multi-colored carpet in my mother's hall, and I keep finding myself saying how I remember something that I didn't think that I had retained. It's because I'd always felt I didn't remember my life until I started this record. I thought that I didn't remember, or lied to myself about remembering, all of my life, because I wanted to be free of the memories. I wanted to have some peace, but now I know what I have done.

A person who lives through extreme trauma doesn't forget anything, ever. Everyone else gets a pardon from childhood. They get to go on. I won't get to go on until I've actually remembered and lived the life that I've denied. Minute by minute, hour by hour, I went away, with my eyes wide open. I'm still in conflict over the going away that I had to do as a child that would always cost me a life that made sense. Now, I'm the one in front of the computer, inventing lives, reliving the past, without knowing how to live. I'm the shadow in every room for myself. I have a hard time being a full physical person.

The hallway of my mother's house would be a holy place for me, in my life's journey. I don't mean holy as a shrine would be built on holy ground. I just mean it's the place where my soul would mostly reside. The hall was important. I would run my fingers down the walls as I walked from sixteen months old, until I finally left home. That hall and I knew each other intimately. I've always found that objects and places are friendlier to me than human life.

My mother's room was down the hall at the end of the doublewide. My room faced another room and a bathroom in that same end of the hall. When I was young, the hall seemed so long. I felt it went on forever. The walls were made up of this brown paneling board that sometimes felt splintery to my fingers.

My mother was a mystery to me. It was after my father left that I knew she was the woman who slept in the room at the end of the hall. I didn't really recognize her being alive until he was gone. She insisted on adopting me from her sister, but I remember her telling me that when I came I didn't want to have anything to do with her. She said I cried from sixteen months until I was three years old when she tried to come near me. I don't know if this was intuition on my part or not, but it certainly was part of what created the dynamic that she and I had.

All I can figure now is that Mother must have always felt that the silent kid that I was was judging her, feeling her energy, and honestly, that would have been too much for me to deal with, too. I wouldn't have done the things she did to cope with the kind of kid that I was, but I think I can understand the pain she must have felt of feeling watched by another human who didn't seem quite well. It must have been eerie, inconvenient, and painful.

I monitored Mother quietly from the time my father left until the time that I walked out of her door at seventeen, but as a little girl my monitoring was completely different than that of the teenage girl who was wearied by her and the mess she had made out of life.

Mother lived in the cave at the end of the hall. That's what I knew of her. The carpeted floor in the hall was the same pattern as the brown, black and white carpet in the living room. Mother's room, her cave, was huge in my child's mind. The windows were covered with foil. A steel fan was always running, along with a personal air conditioner. I remember being small, and her being in the kitchen, while I stood at the entrance of her room, a room that I wasn't allowed to go into. Cool air rushed my face, cigarette smoke filled the air, and there was a death-like mystery reaching out for me. I wondered why it was always so black in there. She had a lamp for reading, but turned it off when she got up to do something.

It's no secret in the lives of those within my mother's house that she wasn't always mentally well. The problem lies in the fact that she was self professed *not mentally well*. It was said throughout my life, *by her*, that she had nervous breakdowns on a few different occasions, but there was a time in my life where her breakdowns cost me too much for me to believe she was ill. In my mind she just wanted someone to save her, and acted out to meet that end.

Some nights I would wake standing at the end of the hall, not knowing how I'd gotten there, not remembering even having left my bed. It was so deeply dark that I understood that it must have been the middle of the night. I'd open my eyes and look around as my breath would catch. How did I get here? I'd wonder. It always happened just like that.

I'd go to bed in my usual state, hoping someone would leave their door open so that I wouldn't be afraid of the dark. No one would leave their door open, though. I felt a terrible panic about that. The boys were long gone to sleep at the back of the house. I was so afraid, but I didn't know what of. I seemed to be afraid of some supernatural occurrence more than I was afraid of any human life. Oddly, I couldn't explain it, but I was also very afraid of myself. I seemed so invisible to me, that I think I was afraid I might disappear all together.

I would wonder how I got there, at the end of the brown paneled hall, my pink flowered nightgown hanging just below my knees. My elbow would bump the wall as I stood close to it. Light would flow in from the great diamond window of the heavy brown door that covered the screen door. My world looked different to me at night.

The heavy drapes weren't ever drawn; they hung with sheers in the middle for decoration. On a moonlit night, I would dare myself to go and stand in the middle of the moonbeams coming through the sheers, and I would dance and twirl to a music that nobody could hear but me, even though I was trembling and terrified. I didn't know what I was doing, but I felt so out of control in my human experience. It was like I was daring myself to live.

I saw the dining room. I saw the entrance to the kitchen. We said hello as I passed from my dance. I don't remember going back to my room on those nights. I just remember wondering how to be. I didn't know if other people did what I did. I didn't know if other girls were as scared to live as I was.

One morning during this time my mother woke up in one of her bad mental days. I do recall her being visibly spooked. She was always so up and down. She was openly afraid of sleep and dreams at different stages of her life. On this particular morning she sat at her big mahogany dining table, making me nervous with her every muttering to my older brother. I was scared of her insanity in my close monitoring of her. I was always waiting to see how she was, as if it would tell me how I was.

Her energy that morning was dark and full of fear.

"I kept hearing one of my children calling my name last night," she fumbled over her coffee and cigarettes, clanging down her yellow lighter.

Jessie just went on eating while Quentin asked her more about it. My heart sank. I felt physically ill. I was, in that moment, so afraid it had been me who was calling her in the night, even though I heard her say that she had gotten up and everyone was asleep. I must have somehow been afraid that I had the power to call out to her telepathically.

I walked up to her, and touched her arm, which spooked her even more. We never touched in our family unless it was dangerous touching. She was wearing one of her blue, silky, flowing gowns.

"Mama, was it me?" I was scared and crazy just like her, and she knew it. "Was it me? Was it me who was calling your name?"

She looked at me a little bewildered, and drew back with pause.

"No, no. It wasn't you. I just said I got up, but everyone was still asleep. It wasn't you, Lizzy." She immediately went back to not seeing me, turning to my brother. She never saw me. She didn't want to see me. I walked away, living in fear of my own quiet contemplation. My soft flowered gown rocked like a bell while I walked away.

3

THE PARTIAL SCREENDOOR

I watched life through the glass top of a partial screendoor. The heavy front door with the diamond shaped window was always open and pushed against the wall. The heavy door was brown; it shut out any light from the outside world. I didn't like that door; it made me feel alone and isolated.

I watched my siblings playing on the porch before school in the morning through the glass of the partial screen door. The glass felt cool against the palms of my hands. I wasn't allowed to join my siblings on the porch. They were waiting for their schoolbus to come. I wasn't old enough to attend school yet, but I yearned to attend as I watched my siblings so intently. All of the children were in an elementary school together. Leslie and Quentin would be going to different schools the following year probably.

When I explain this part above, I'm unsure of my age standing in front of the glass and watching the others. I think I was about three. It had to be when my father still lived at home. I know this because my sister went to school from his new home after he left us.

The partial screendoor still stands in my mother's home today. There's no reason for me to believe it was ever altered or removed. The times I've gone back it was certainly still there. The creaking quality that it had was unique for me.

Some mornings I would get up and I would have slept too late and missed watching my older siblings go to school. I remember coming down the hall sometimes and the world being so quiet. From the start, I didn't like the silence of their being already gone; the absence of them made me want to get lost in myself.

I would sometimes stand at the end of the hall, turn my body around, putting my back to the screendoor and the living room, and squat with my face between my legs to look at the room upside down. My need to twist reality was natural to me for as long as I can remember. I entertained myself with an upside down world. The carpet was thick with various shades of black and brown mixed with a bright white. There was also the round brown stool that I would sometimes drag over to the door to watch people passing by when I would become too tired to stand any longer. I don't remember the hallway being frightening for me yet.

My father must have left just before I started kindergarten, because when I finally started kindergarten I was frightened and I didn't want to go. I was on the other side of the screendoor on the porch with Jessie, alone. The school zones changed for the older kids, Leslie was gone, and no one took me to school on the first day to get me oriented. I was told to get on the bus with Jessie and go. I remember being there with him, but I don't remember what he said or did. The porch was an empty, scary place, in my mind then.

I woke up one morning in my kindergarten year and I didn't know what time it was. I was sure I'd missed the school bus. I didn't know where Jessie was. I don't remember where my mother would have been. Everyone had gone, but the going was a part of that world that was multidimensional around me. There were my private worlds, and there was my life with the others around me, my family.

Not frightened, but disoriented, I tried to figure out what I was supposed to do that day. I didn't want to be out of place. I desperately needed to be where I was supposed to be. My body felt heavy, exhausted even. My attempt to be okay inside was overwhelming for me.

Frantically I looked around the room, thought of what to wear, and grabbed a pair of pants with a very deep split that was obvious in them. I reached for a button up multicolored shirt, and put on my torn tennis shoes. I scooted down the hall to my screendoor to see if I could see other kids going to the bus stop that was now at the end of the driveway of the house of the girl across the street. I didn't see any other kids, so I wandered my porch and yard trying to think of what to do. I was nervous and stressed.

Finally I saw other kids and a relief poured over me. I had been sweating with the grief and disorientation I was feeling. My brain was thinking joyfully that I was going to be able to feel okay again. I was so happy as I took my seat on the bus. I was delighted to belong there in the trembling seat.

I spent the day being terrorized by the other students in my class about my split pants. I couldn't run or do anything in PE without my split being obvious, but this didn't bother me at all. I was just so happy to have found out where I belonged so that I didn't have to be out of place. My mind was confusing enough without the additional stress of being disoriented.

Later in life I would stand at that door. My ages at the various stages of standing there aren't important. Just the thoughts are important, now, I think. I stood there watching Cindy, the little girl my age across the street, walking with her mother. I often saw her, this Cindy, playing outside and her mother coming out to check on her, or see what she needed. Her mother sometimes brought her things. I watched the two of them. I studied what they were doing. I wondered about those people a lot of the time when I was alone. They were fascinating to me. I was like a scientist studying human life.

I wondered about lots of things, really, when it came to the mother and daughter I watched. Does Cindy's mother hit her repeatedly, and then go silent, I wondered? Is Cindy afraid to sleep alone because of the bad people that come in the night? Does Cindy feel like she could be sucked into another universe? Is Cindy afraid to live but trying to keep herself alive because she's afraid to die all at the same time?

Mostly, the pair, Cindy and her mother, looked very happy, though, but I knew enough to know not to believe in that too fully. They did look pleasant at least. I did wish I could know what it was like to feel like Cindy, but I never wished I could be her specifically.

With me and Cindy, I wondered, even as a small child, what caused such a huge contrast in our different existences. Honestly, though, I'm kind of proud to say that I accepted even then that she had her life and I had mine. I just had a sense of knowing I was in the right body and in the right time. I can't tell you how I knew this, but I did.

I just looked at Cindy as a specimen of study.

That's what life was to me, a study. It, life, just seemed to be what it was. I can still feel my forehead and palms against the cool glass of the partial screendoor when I think about it. What a feeling, to have truly lived and felt, and seen...even as a child.

4

GRETCHEN

I was looking for Gretchen. I looked under the bed for her. I looked in the closet for her. I looked in my clothes drawers for her. I looked in every place you could think of when you're four years old to look for something valuable that's lost.

I remember thinking, "I should check in my blankets one more time." I kept imagining that I'd move the covers and suddenly she would appear. I was desperate to find her.

I wandered through the doublewide, searching as I walked. I knew I never took Gretchen out of my room, but maybe, somehow, this time I had.

I heard the noise going on in the house, people's voices, boxes shifting with clamor; I didn't put it all together in my mind. Where was Gretchen?

I looked on the front porch. I walked up and down the red clay driveway. I went back inside and traced my steps back down the hallway to my room, but there was no Gretchen. I sat on my bed, confused and bewildered. I didn't know quite what to do.

Gretchen was my rubber baby doll. She took baths with me, and I dressed her for bed so that she could sleep with me. I slept with Gretchen every night. I told Gretchen things, but I can't remember what those things were. I loved Gretchen and Gretchen loved me.

I decided again, in my small brown room, with my feet dangling in the dark part of the day, that I should do another search for Gretchen. I looked under the bed. I looked in blankets. I was inside my closet when I heard a noise that filled me with a wild sort of sinking feeling.

"Do you have everything? This is our last trip to the dump today," the man's voice rang out loud and clear. My mother had gotten a friend to help her clean out the house after Dad had moved out.

I climbed up on the bed so that I could look out the back window. I stood with my nose to the screen and my fingers gripping the frame. My window looked out over the back porch and yard. I saw the truck full of trash bags and miscellaneous debris. I kept thinking, Gretchen couldn't be there. How could Gretchen be there? Gretchen always stays in my room.

I climbed off my bed and started running through the kitchen to the back door. When you're little, it is a run! I paused at the door as Jessie looked in on me through the glass. He had a smirky look on his face.

"I saw you looking for something. It was that doll, I bet." I just stared at him.

"She threw her in the truck for the dump. She said you didn't need it anymore!" He sounded hard, like he didn't mind telling me the hateful news.

I backed up a little. He came inside and went into his room. I just felt myself staring down. I didn't know how I was supposed to act. My chin had fallen to my chest. I felt the skin on skin connection. I walked to my room.

When I got to my room, I climbed up on my bed again. I peered out at the over-flowing truck that was headed for the dump. I asked myself if Gretchen could really be in that truck. Could that be real? Could Gretchen be there? Why Gretchen?

I turned and peered around my room. I slid down onto the edge of the bed with my feet dangling. The room was getting darker as the sun was going down. I had my gown from the morning on the floor in the corner. My brown dresser had randomly opened drawers. My hollow brown door was closed.

I sat there trying to figure out why Gretchen, with all the other things in my room? I had lots of stuffed animals, and other things of that nature, too. It actually came to mind that the woman, that was the mother, had come into my room and just picked up that particular thing—had picked up Gretchen. But why that thing? Why Gretchen?

I couldn't make out, if it was purposeful, the taking of Gretchen. I was little, my mind went to her taking Gretchen deliberately, but my mind could only know that there must have been a reason, and I didn't understand the reason. My mind, at that stage, couldn't think, "Well, she was taking what I loved the most." But the notion was an unsaid reality, somewhere in my psyche.

I felt overcome with this sinking feeling in my stomach. I imagined Gretchen was under my covers. I would lift my light green bed cover several times thinking the next time I lifted it I would see Gretchen. I opened the closet over and over, expecting to see Gretchen each time I opened it. I kept peering under the bed. I was singing her name softly just tiny enough to be heard.

"I love you Gretchen. Won't you come out now and play with me?"

She didn't come out, though, and no amount of peering under the bed, lifting covers, or opening and closing my closet door was going to bring her back to me. She was gone forever.

I had an emotional connection to Gretchen after my father left. I lived in a world that I created for the both of us. It meant something to me, my life with Gretchen. Gretchen was like me, in my mind.

When I took my bath that night, I pretended Gretchen was with me in the tub. Gretchen was funny in the tub and she could always pee after she was full of water. I was always in the tub alone in the evenings with her. Someone would run a bath, and tell me to go get in it. Aunt May ran my bath sometimes, when she was in town.

"Don't be afraid of the water, Gretchen. I'll take care of you," my little voice would explain.

"Don't worry. The glass door won't fall in. It just did that once," referring to the glass bathtub doors.

"I could never pee that much," I would talk to her, like always.

I lay in bed that night, worried about Gretchen being in some dark and lonely place. I was eaten up with the fact that I had let her be taken. If I had only hid her, I thought to myself. If I had only not let anyone see that I loved her. The guilt was so profound, for me, and the suffering was so deep, that I always carried the loss of Gretchen with me, even into counseling in my adult life.

Every night, for I don't know how long, I worried about what I had let happen to Gretchen. Gretchen was scared and alone. Gretchen had no one to love her, and it was my fault. It was my fault, what had happened to Gretchen.

I didn't cry about wanting my doll back. My soul cried because

I had not guarded Gretchen's life. Instead of living her life with me, she now lived alone, in fear, in isolation. I had not wanted what had happened to me to happen to Gretchen. I'd wanted Gretchen to have a different life.

5

THE HOSPITAL

I think I was five. I lay on the stretcher in my yellow nightgown and green socks. My stomach hurt. My mother and Aunt May were whispering between themselves. The lights in the room were turned down, and I remember the groans of the people around me. I had a shrinking feeling. I didn't know what happened, or why I was there in the hospital. It seemed like I just woke up to that world, wondering what was going on, and why I was there.

I looked at *the mother*, or that's how I referred to her in my conception. She…, that lady, she is the mother, *"we call her the mother."* I wasn't used to my mother being in my focus yet. I was still coming into this new world of reality where she would loom larger than anything else.

That person, my mother, shifted into different energies. I didn't understand, or I wasn't able to make out all of her faces yet. My breath was shallow when she turned her attention to me. Looking at her made my stomach churn.

Doctor Summers came up to us, a doctor who had become my general doctor. He was tall, fit, with jet black, graying hair. I didn't mind him coming up to me. What I did notice, in learning about my mother, was that when the doctor came up to us, she showed one of her many different faces.

Mother's hands were very big in my mind. She'd never touched me with them unless she was angry, but when the doctor came up, she suddenly put one of her hands on my back and started stroking me softly. I didn't like her touching me. I squirmed. I seemed to be always more comfortable in general without people touching me, and when she touched me, I was keenly aware that something just wasn't right about it.

"How is everything, Mrs. Elliot? I'm very sorry that you had to come so late tonight." He was putting his stethoscope into his ears to listen to my heart.

"Oh, I don't mind anything, as long as my baby's okay." Her kind sounds didn't register with anything I'd experienced before. She was clearly acting like something that wasn't her. She leaned into me, as if to make sure she kept the doctor's focus on her at all times.

"How are you tonight, Lizzy?" he asked with the kindest smile. He was trying to look at me directly, when my mother touched his arm and began lamenting her concern for me.

"She's been in bad shape tonight," she was answering for me, very parasitically needing his attention, though I didn't understand it so fully back then. "She's been throwing up, I can't get the fever down, and all she has in the world is me and her Aunt May to care for her. It's very hard."

Summers cut her off. "I understand, Mrs. Elliot. I'm very sorry about the hard time you're having. We'll get a room for Lizzy and try to get this fever under control."

He tried to speak to me again. "Lizzy, does this hurt?" He was pushing a little at my stomach, but I didn't get to answer him before my mother cut in again.

"She's in terrible pain and I just don't know what we're going to do. We've tried everything." She was presenting things in a way that was curious. She was acting so concerned. I knew that she wasn't. She switched all of the time. That part I was getting clearly by this time.

I don't know what I would have said to the doctor anyway. I was very uncomfortable with having the mother so physically near. I was very caught up in the nuances of her behaviors and the different sounds in her voice. Also, I didn't feel much physical pain. I had a disconnected factor. Strangely, I think I was also following the mother's lead on how to act about the pain, because I didn't know how to feel it. I did apparently have a very high fever.

Mother went on and on with the doctor, inappropriately telling him about her life. She kept saying how hard the divorce was on me. It seemed like maybe she wanted him to feel sorry for her, through using me. I wasn't in touch enough yet to be embarrassed by her antics. I would eventually understand that she acted differently when we were around other people. Her eyes told the same stories differently sometimes.

I'd overhear her telling things about me to a friend on the phone. That's how I actually learned a lot about my own life, through listening to her on the phone with a friend. Sometimes she would talk to someone all afternoon, chainsmoking cigarettes, while lounging on a very expensive multicolored couch, and having me bring her things so she didn't have to get up.

"Lizzy, empty this ashtray." She would be speaking kindly to me like anyone else's mother, but I knew it was for the person on the other end of the line to hear. She didn't want people who knew her to know how she was with me.

I was in hospitals a lot. There were family stories of my becoming ill with terrible fevers in the night, many times over, and the trips to the emergency room. I was a sickly child. I had ear infections, tubes, and more extensive ear surgeries on a few occasions. I'm sure my ear troubles contributed to my dreamy childhood state.

One time while I was in the hospital one of Mother's friends gave me a dog that had two ears on each side of his head. I can't tell you how funny I thought it was that this white knitted poodle dog had a hidden set of smaller ears under his larger outer ears. I lay in the bed, in partial light, alone, and marveled at the dog I'd received. Through the years I'd show that dog to people and ask them what was different about the dog, and delight in waiting for them to realize it was the double ears.

I still have that dog in a keepsake box today. I don't know why I've kept it.

6

AUNT MAY

I remember a Crayola Crayons themed record player I got as a Christmas gift at the age of four. I had gotten it on Christmas Eve. It was the old style record player that children had in the early seventies, a suitcase-like plastic box that opened to a bright white turntable, and a little wide white arm that you put on a record to have it magically play.

I loved the Crayola record player, and I marveled at the record I played over and over again: "Rhinestone Cowboy" by Glen Campbell. I remember the other side of the record had the song "Country Boy." I knew all of the words by heart.

Also, this particular Christmas Eve, I received a "Playdoh Barber Shop" set that I'd seen on TV a hundred times. I begged for that Barber set to my Aunt May, who stayed with us sometimes, and she liked to please me.

Aunt May loved little girls, and I was told that she didn't particularly like little boys. She came from a time when men and women were very separate, and she'd never had children of her own. She was very old, and the boys, my four brothers, were very wild.

I sat happily with my Aunt May, who was actually my father's Aunt, and with the mother. I know the mother was there, but she and I didn't interact. I think I observed her friendly manner with Aunt May, but with my mother every happy communication with others always seemed not quite right, suspect, or for a hidden reason. The energy in the room with the mother always seemed wrong.

I understood, in later years, that the mother never liked my Aunt May. The mother was wounded. She didn't trust anyone.

That Christmas Eve I laughed in front of the tree and played my record player. It was only the three of us. I don't know why we were alone. My father was gone, for sure, at this time. Maybe the older kids were at his new home. I was sick to my stomach a lot in those days. Maybe the mother said I was too ill to go that Christmas Eve night.

My mother and Aunt May sat at the mahogany dining table talking about what grownups talked about. In the double wide, the dining room met with the living room at one end of it. A Christmas tree with hideously beautiful silver tinsel reached all the way to the ceiling, in the middle of the two rooms, joining them against the wall.

I surveyed the room as my record played over and over a short distance from the two women. The multi-colored carpet felt soft underneath my fingers when I would allow myself to fall to the ground from a bounding, dizzying, spin. Spinning was my way of dancing.

I liked Christmas, then, when I was little. I liked Aunt May. Somehow, when Aunt May was there in the early years, I was a little more relaxed. Aunt May was a buffer to things that I can't remember, things on the edge of my mind that I'm unwilling to see yet. I didn't learn to hide from my Aunt May until I was a few years older, but I hope that wherever she is, she has forgiven me for that.

Aunt May had a room across the hall from mine at the other end of the mother's double wide. She made me snacks when she was around, which was nice because the mother didn't ever think about feeding anyone. Aunt May let me come into her room when I was afraid of the dark at night.

When she wasn't there, I just did my normal survival routine. I hid in my closet, or in the hall linen closet. I liked quiet dark places, places that were safe, because they could only fit me.

I would hide when the mother would start to scream at Aunt May in later times. The mother was openly verbally abusive to my Aunt May. I think Aunt May was asked to come stay with us to help out because of the large number of children, and both parents worked. When our father left, Aunt May did not. She still stayed with us most of the time.

I remember Christmases later in life when my mother didn't let Aunt May come out of her room. I was conflicted about her not coming out. All the treasures I'd made for her through the year were courageously wrapped in construction paper for my Aunt May to come out and open. I eventually started taking her things to her room for her to open.

I learned to hate Christmas, but for more reasons than the mother's treatment of Aunt May. Christmas was just one of those bad pictures that repeated itself because of the mother's disturbed emotions.

It confused me that Aunt May just sat in her room and cried on Christmas. I didn't understand the tears. I just wanted her to stop crying.

7

CHURCH

I haven't had a lot of rage in my life, though some therapists have said I should find it. I never look back and blame the people who have most damaged my life for the things that they've done. I don't feel damaged. My eyes have been opened to life in a unique way, and for that I must give thanks.

Ultimately, I think that the people around me, in both the good and the bad that they've done, have just been trying to figure out their own soul's journey, in their own time, and in their own way. Carrying a physical body is a scary thing for all of us. It's temporary and confusing.

In my small Southern community, the population was made up mostly of Southern Baptists. There were various types of Baptists that I understood when I was a little girl.

There was the wonderful, wholesome, God fearing Baptist whose faith could not be shaken, and there didn't have to be a reason for them to believe in their Heavenly Father. They just did.

There they were, on their porches on Sunday after church, talking about how good it was to be alive in the hands of God. They were eating fried chicken and rocking in rocking chairs. Whatever went on in life, they were never wearied. They just stayed in the peaceful state they were in. I would sit on the edge of the steps, when in their company, and just be.

Their energy never hurt me. These people I knew weren't grabbing for my soul. I didn't need anyone grabbing for my soul. I needed to be able to watch the world evenly and collect my personal data. My snapshots of them were easy, but I saw early on that there weren't a lot of these people around me.

Though I appreciated this type of Christian very much, I did not wish to be one of them. It might be because I instinctively knew that I wasn't one of them. I think the knowing came from the fact that I'd already seen so many monstrous adult things that my brain was automatically introspective.

I couldn't have rocked on those porches, sending thoughts into the hands of the unknown. I was too awake for that, and once you're awake, you just can't go to sleep again. Being awake was my journey. The people around me woke me up. I'm not saying that this type of Christian lived a simple life; it was just a different kind of life than the path I had to take. I found this type of Christian's wisdom to be profound, and the depth of their love to be extraordinarily pure. I actually thought they were beyond me in the journey, because they could be at peace on the planet.

The next type of Baptist that I understood in childhood was the struggling-with- faith Baptist, the people who were less free internally, but felt it was Sunday and they should be at church, so they were there, before going off to deal with the struggles of everyday life. It seemed like these Christians carried great burdens, wanted to believe in God, made their efforts, but life was just too heavy for them to believe in any kind of happiness.

I steered myself away from this type. They couldn't see me; they were no threat to me. They were completely oblivious of anything outside of themselves and their problems with existence.

Then, last, in my child's mind, were the Baptists who were too concerned with the lives of others. These people, especially the ladies, made life painful for me.

"How's your mother?" one would say. Even as a child I knew they didn't like my mother. "I hear she's got a new boyfriend. Now, honestly, how many times has your mother been married?"

I was six. I didn't know. I just felt numb, wiggled in my chair, and shrugged my shoulders. These women all smelt like soap that hadn't been washed off. I guess it was their perfumes. I don't wear any kind of perfume even to this day. The smell is overpowering to me. I feel I should smell like myself.

"Oh, come now, you must have some idea. Well, what's her new boyfriend do for a job? You know, does he work somewhere?" Her eyes would turn to the ladies around us to see what their reactions to her questions were.

Everything goes blank here.

My mother made me go to church with Quentin's young soon-to-be wife, starting at the age of six. Quentin and Laura were seventeen at the time. Laura lived around the block and had gone to school with my older siblings. She came from a group of people who I believed were obsessed with righteousness. I say this because they attacked my mother, and her life, verbally in front of me. The evidence of their self-righteousness was there, in my face, and there was no way to escape the reality of it. They thought they were kind to me, and on my side, when it came to having to live with my mother, their singling me out, making me feel ashamed and different, wasn't kind to me.

This group of people made sure I was picked up on every occasion of church. They remembered me at Christmas. They whispered loudly about my mother in front of me. They provoked me with questions to see how I'd respond. My mother was the bad lady in the neighborhood, and they were the ones with the eternal place with God.

I'd be my crazy fucking mother any day if I had to make a choice between their lives and hers. Any God they knew was no God to me.

"Have you found Jesus, child?" The preacher's voice starts out kindly.

"Well," I think to myself, with a shudder, "I just don't know." I shake wordlessly in front of the questioner on the platform. All eyes are on him.

"Have you found Jesus, child?" He repeats it again, but with more emphasis this time.

I fumble through the question in my mind. What I want to say is that I feel God in the closet when I'm hiding. It feels like someone's watching me, but I turn to see who it is, and no one's there.

I mull it over in my mind. Have I found him? Where is the savior? Savior seems like a cold word. My heart just beats faster.

"You're not too young to know our Heavenly Father," the preacher's tone gets hotter.

I think to myself again, "Yes…, I know, you must be right…, but I don't want to know about pain and fear. I don't want to know about the fiery depths of hell, where there is no water to quench your thirst. I don't want to die now, you've convinced me of that, but I don't want to live here with all of you either." My head aches just a little above my left temple.

"Have you found Jesus, child!?" the preacher's face grows red. His voice is raised to the congregation. "If you are at an age of consciousness, then you are at an age to burn in the fiery pits of hell!" His voice goes through the room like a storm that has just landed.

My chest shakes a little. I am completely conscious. I want to go to the bathroom. I ponder in my seat how to live and how to die.

My tiny, pleated, blue pastel skirt is no comfort for me. The pew is cold on my bottom. My plastic church shoes hurt my feet. The church's bible is enormous and heavy in my hands. My eyes search around the room, trying to understand the others. They have Jesus, they say. They say they know God.

Laura had no idea what her surrounding religious world did to me, or the fear it built inside of me. Laura was a person who always tried to be good to me. There was also a particular pastor who was very good to me in my early life. No one meant for this to happen. I'd feel so ashamed if they read this now, and felt that I did not love them, even though I felt this way. I have to believe that they tried to love me.

My mind would weep if my physical body wouldn't. There was nothing good in reality. Not in a pew, holding a heavy bible, wishing the world would just obliterate, and being forced to live in a faith that could never be my own.

8

KINDERGARTEN

I remember a floating feeling about Kindergarten. I didn't know if I even wanted to go to school by that time; I had been knocked unsteady by the changes and the loneliness in our lives. I think I must have learned to think it was a good idea to have something to do in life, to pass the time, to not always stand in front of the partial screendoor. I think that something inside of me knew to push forward, to just wade through it all, and see if something good might happen away from the mother.

Miss Meyer was my teacher, and she was very young and kind. We had name charts, we sat at desks, we went to special area, we did everything kids did, I guess, and I just floated along like I was supposed to.

I wanted to play with the other children, and I don't remember anyone being specifically unkind to me, but things were out of alignment somehow. Each day when the children dispersed to the designated play areas, like the pretend house or the pretend store, they seemed to disperse with me lagging behind.

I would go to the different areas and try to play with the other children, but they seemed to always be doing something already planned out that didn't have room for an added person.

In the beginning I would go to an area and the children would let me know that I'd gone to the wrong place. They were right. I was floaty. It seemed like I didn't understand where I was supposed to be. Looking back, I might have appeared to have a cognitive problem. I know my poor hearing made me feel confused a lot of the time.

I know that I must have looked different to the other children, too, in my hand-me-downs of older brothers' clothes, or just whatever I'd thrown together for school. My mother didn't think much about appearances when it came to her children's clothes, and neither did I. There was no harm in her sending me to school in whatever, I guess. I was little. She came from a world where that kind of thing just didn't matter. Everyone was poor. I don't think she understood how kids were stigmatized in that way.

I did have a hard time as I got older, and sometimes I had no coat, or I had to continue rotating two pair of pants. Mother would dress herself in three hundred dollar ball gowns, traipse around the house in them, and brag about how she would only buy the best for herself, while I walked around in holey shoes.

I have a flash of memory of one time in kindergarten when Miss Meyer got really mad at me, which she rarely did. I never knew how to respond to other humans in my floaty state.

"Lizzy Elliot! We are calling your mother! You will be missing the bus today!" Her voice heightened and her cheeks tanned more than her normal olive color. She was one of the prettiest women I'd ever seen. Her frame was delicate, and I remember her hair matched the caramel color of her skin.

"You just march on over and sit against the wall by my desk, while I dismiss the rest of the class, young lady!" I remember the lines and angles of her body; her hip bones were pronounced when she walked. She always wore these button-down silky blouses, with dress slacks and heels. I felt like a monster in comparison to her angelic qualities and piercing brown eyes.

I walked over and sat beside her desk against the wall. There was no dialogue, because I didn't say anything. I sat with baggy jeans and an ugly buttoned down shirt, with my knees drawn up to my chest. I put my face in my hands on my knees, and I remember pretending, *"They can't see me, if I can't see them."* I felt elation, or relief, in that idea that they couldn't see me. I would pretend that I was in my own little world, as my eyes stared at the concrete floor between my legs.

Maybe if I called Miss Meyer up today, which I think I might, maybe she would tell me what I was in those days. Maybe kindly Miss Meyer could help me remember me. But, I'd hate to frighten her; teachers are funny, private, and self protective with information. I don't blame them for it, of course, with all life's scrutiny.

"Lizzy, are you okay?" The sound of her voice was generally light, and the vibrations of it seemed so positive. I think she might have been happy about life, though she seemed like a lonely woman to me, or maybe she just still had this tremendous belief in the happiness life could bring.

Again, "Lizzy, how are you today?" I remember her perfectly manicured hands on the front of her thighs as she squatted a little to speak to me. And she always did speak to me. She always let me know that she could see me, that I really was alive.

I hear her voice, but I never hear my own. I ponder and I ponder and I ponder, but thank you anyway, Miss Meyer, for seeing me, and for asking me how I was, in those strange and innocent days.

9

TWO TEACHERS

"Miss Elliot, you'll have to work faster than that!" Mrs. Page stood like a regal queen in the doorway of my sixth grade English class. She was watching the class take notes from the overhead, and waiting to see who needed to be done so that she could go on to the next transparency.

"Yes, Ma'am," I stuttered, embarrassed. Everyone was looking at me. I felt the sweat that had developed on my forehead. Whenever classes in school did this kind of group activity, the activity always proved publicly to be too big of a challenge for me. Everyone saw how *not smart* I was.

"Miss Elliot, you've got to get a move on!" That was Mrs. Page. She was poised, she smelled good, and I thought she must be rich because of all her jewelry. I was a child. I wanted Mrs. Page to like me. She was a tall, elegant black woman. I hung around her desk before class, even though I never completed any assignments.

"Yes, Ma'am," I was sweating; she was harder on me than usual today. Her exasperation let me know that I needed very specifically to do exactly what the other children were doing. I couldn't do it! I was nervous and afraid, all of the time.

When I hung around Mrs. Page's desk, at this poverty stricken black and white school, she did not take the time to notice me. She had a very isolating, very formal, "Good afternoon, Miss Elliot," for me. Something in her voice let me know, even at twelve, that this was an elementary good greeting, that it would have been beneath her not to have given it, and so she would. She was too classy to have not been correct in her manners.

I did notice, without judgment, that she always had a crowd of little black girls around her desk; her voice was different with them. I wished at night that my skin could be black, or that maybe skin color wouldn't matter, and maybe she could like me too. I noticed that Mrs. Page had two ways of being.

Her voice came down like the voice of a God, or like a hammer blacking you out of the masses, setting you apart: "Miss Elliot, you...., cannot..., copy..., one..., word..., at a time!" she boomed.

Me, my body was trembling. I dropped my pencil as the class stared and laughed at me behind their hands. She was right, I thought, "I do copy one word at a time." I knew she was right. I would get a word, write it down, and then look for where I'd gotten the last word from to get the next word. I could not do a sentence at a time. I didn't know what to do, though. They made me go to school. It was the law. I was forced to go to school and I had to survive that life, along with surviving the life with my mother.

I was sweating, hunkered at my desk, staring at Mrs. Page; her eyes had this calm, regal glare to them. Maybe I blacked out, but I don't remember anything after that except two things: I never went to Mrs. Page's desk again, wishing my skin was black so that she would talk to me; and I have never again copied anything in my life without hearing her voice in my head: "Miss Elliot, you...., cannot..., copy..., one..., word..., at a time!"

Mrs. Page has never left me. I'm still always afraid of my own judgment, and unsure in any academic environment. I always feel people are watching me, in any setting where you have to do what other people are doing. I'm always the last person to finish any test in a testing room. I'm just too unsure of myself. I did battle my way through to a degree eventually, but the psychological cost was more than I can ever express.

There was another teacher who affected me that year, in a very different way. Mrs. Landon was a robust, beautiful black woman whom I did not approach for comfort the way that I did with Mrs. Page.

I stepped into Mrs. Landon's room and something in me turned off. I didn't have any feelings about the world around me when I stepped over the threshold of her room.

I came to school every day of my childhood worried, like worry blacks you out into another dimension. I can't explain my sudden tremblings. I had my mother on me. I had the fact that my life was nothing, because I couldn't do what the other kids were doing in school. Looking back, I can't believe what stress can do to a person. It makes you feel the line between life and death. Fear and stress make you see, it's this world or that!

I stepped over the threshold to Mrs. Landon's room, and all the pain that I felt inside dissipated. It was like there was a mystical energy in the room around her. Putting my foot into the door of her room felt like stepping into my closet in my bedroom to hide, or like the feeling I got when I climbed up into the linen closet where no one could find me.

Being in Mrs. Landon's room taught me something, it showed me something that I'd not quite yet understood in the physical world. Mrs. Landon was the first person to show me that some people had spiritual energies that were stronger than negative realities, that there was something more in the world than just the "Do you live or do you die?" question.

Mrs. Landon taught me, without her knowing it, to take a spiritual journey, to seek out others like her. Eventually that knowledge would save my life.

Mrs. Landon never had a conversation with me that I can remember. She never even touched me that I can recall, but she had something unexplainable going on around her. I will always respect what she brought to my life with her simple presence in it.

I never rushed to her room. I had other thoughts. I just went, and I would feel the breath leave my body like I'd been carrying it locked in all of my life, when my foot crossed over the threshold of her room.

"Miss Elliot, Miss Elliot, now you stand up a little straighter, please." It was Chorus, and we were getting ready for a performance of some kind. When she spoke, even to gain order, you didn't have to be confused about the meaning behind the sound in her voice, and she was soft by no means. Mrs. Landon was a powerful, straight and orderly person. Her voice was joyful in a way that wasn't joyful for purpose; it felt like her voice was whispering underneath what she was actually saying.

It felt like Mrs. Landon's whispery, underneath voice was saying: "We're all in this life together now. You're not separate from me. This is a dance we've all come to. It's not harder for you than it is for me!

You just have to bear down! Life isn't meant to be easy. Let's just see how strong you are, and what we can do with it! I love you. It is right to love you, and by God, I can see you! Don't look back! Nothing's behind you. Don't look back. Catch your breath now. Release, yes, release. Don't look back!"

Her voice was strong and forthright. She never had a doubt.

"Nothing's got you…, but you…, now you let go of that!"

Her underneath whispery voice shook me all over.

I will always love Mrs. Landon. I don't know how she did it, how she made me feel like I was somebody alive in a journey. I don't know how she gave me the reality of myself in a spiritual world.

I didn't float with her; I felt my spirit beyond my skin. For the first time I knew that I really existed, that I was alive, not just this floaty thing that drifted, while everyone else was somehow real. I had lived my life wanting to be imaginary; that's what I understood to be safe. To admit that I wasn't imaginary was somehow too painful to accept, but Mrs. Landon changed that.

I've wondered a lot of my life if anyone else heard Mrs. Landon's *underneath* voice, a voice that made me wonder what my own *underneath* voice might be.

I loved Mrs. Landon, I loved her calmness. In Mrs. Landon's room, I knew I was really with her, with a greater universe, and I'd never felt like I was with anyone or anything. The woman was like magic to me. I wish her the best in all of her life.

10

DARRELL

But neither Mrs. Landon nor anyone else could have prepared me for Darrell.

It was at the start of that sixth grade year at the very poverty-stricken multi-racial school. All the kids found fault with each other. All the kids found fault with themselves. I wasn't alone in my negative circumstances, this I knew. My pain may have been more extreme, more constant, more calculated, than most, but we all had pain enough to spare. It wasn't the psychological age, it was the survival age, and we did that, we did the best that we could.

I remember a little black boy who waited for me every day by my locker. His name was Darrell, and he was very angry with me. He would come up to me seething, "I hate you, Elliot, I hate you!!" I would huddle into my locker. I was a mousy kid. I didn't know that middle school could be so threatening. I had been excited about something new in my life, before it began.

Darrell would follow me to class, "I'm gonna get you, Elliot, I'm going to kill you!" I would go and sit down with him circling my chair and chanting. I didn't know that it wasn't normal for someone to do this to me, after the life I'd lived at home. It seemed like an extension of what to expect, in the journey.

"Say something, Elliot! You know I'm gonna get you! It's just a matter of time!" he sneered in my face.

I never said anything. I'd never even spoken a word to him. I didn't know why he chose me to do this to every day. It just seemed like an extension of things that I didn't understand.

"Look at me, Elliot," he shouted, and I looked at him. His eyes didn't make me think that he was bad. He seemed to be in some kind of pain. His eyes were deep and dark; they reminded me of my own eyes.

"What, you think you can look at me, Elliot? You're dead!" He would then run out of the room. He was a small, wiry little boy, quite cute. I remember people around whispering, "Why is she afraid of him?" Now, looking back, I wonder, why didn't he want to kill the kids that were whispering, not that I wished any ill will on them, but why did he choose me?

As far as why I was afraid of Darrell, well, that part is easy. I'd been taught to submit to the pain and needs of others from the start of my life. There was no way in the world I could do anything but wish him away, and there was no one in the world that I felt that I could tell what was happening to me.

Darrell finally made physical contact at my locker, one early school morning. He ran up screaming obscenities, and started punching me like he was a man, pinning me up against the black painted lockers. I just huddled as close to my locker as I could until he stopped. All the people standing around didn't seem to even notice what he had done.

I needed to throw up. I was dizzy, and I felt like I was vibrating I was trembling so badly. It didn't hurt really, the punching. It felt like it did when my mother hit me; I just went away inside of my head. The pain was of being the one that's chosen for that, the one that gets to live in a constant terror. The expectation of pain is exhausting. Tears streamed down my reddened face as a release of pressure, not because I had a feeling human heart.

The last of Darrell came when he followed me to class one day.

"Today's the day, Elliot!" he shouted as he jumped on me. He beat my face and my stomach until I fell to the ground. Two teachers had to pull him off of me. Of course, no one knew why he did it. It was this unexplainable thing. But maybe, I thought, it was just because he could see that I was something bad, a person that you just did that kind of thing to.

"Miss Elliot, were you and Darrell having trouble?" The overweight male principal in a tight gray suit was filling out paperwork as he asked me questions.

"No sir."

"Are you sure? Darrell's not explaining to us why he was so upset."

I just sat quietly as he groaned and sent me on to the nurse.

Christmas was around the corner, and I was glad about the school break.

I'm not upset about Darrell and what happened back then. I thought Darrell was someone like me. I actually wonder what happened to him, and if he made it out of the hard life that we had to live. I hope he did. One of my friends suggested once that maybe Darrell had a crush on me, and didn't know how to think about that. I just laughed, and thought, maybe, but maybe not. Whatever the case, Darrell had something he was desperately trying to work out.

11

FOOD

Food was a funny thing in our family. Food was a gift and privilege to those well liked, and mostly reserved for grownups. On every occasion, Mother always insisted that the children not eat until after the adults were finished. This went for all of my siblings, too.

Even if she didn't let you in the kitchen all day to get your breakfast, children weren't allowed, even on holidays, to come get food while adults were still around the table. Sometimes the adults sat around the table for hours, eating, talking and smoking. I remember many days starving until well into the afternoon and evening.

Our lives were made up of peanut butter sandwiches and huge Southern meals when my mother would occasionally decide to make one, or the traditional lima beans and rice which was sometimes available on the stove. Mostly, though, our lives were made up of peanut butter sandwiches, and there's nothing wrong with that.

It's the attitudes and messages about food that were disturbing, like when we were really small and we weren't allowed to eat until Mother had the inclination to feed us.

As I got older, as everyone got older, and every so often she would cook a big meal, the rules changed. I personally had to wait until given specific permission to eat anything Mother cooked, while my brothers would walk in right in front of me and take whatever they wanted to eat, and be encouraged to take what they wanted. She would seem so proud of herself while watching them enjoy the food she cooked.

I wasn't starving; it's just that I wasn't significant in the food importance order. *I could wait! I could finish doing some task! I could do whatever,* while she encouraged the world around me to come eat.

I would stumble in the shadows of the kitchen I had to clean. I crept around slowly, waiting for her to scream, "What the hell are you doing in my kitchen!? Get out of my kitchen! I worked all day to cook that meal! Just get the hell out of there and leave my stuff alone!"

I never drank milk, when I was little. Jessie loved milk, though. Mother would scream, "You kids are drinking all of my milk! Leave my milk alone! I didn't buy it for you, goddamn it!" She would stand in her silky gowns, cigarette dangling from one hand, surveying the refrigerator.

"There's never any bread around here!" she would scream habitually, when bread was most of the time all we had to eat.

Then there were times in our lives when she hardly cooked anything. There were also the times when she was sleeping at a boyfriend's house, and Jessie, Brent and I were left to figure out how to eat when there was no food in the house. This happened quite a bit after Dad left. I remember on occasion her picking us up to go meet a boyfriend after she would have been gone for days. When we got to the place where this person lived, we'd see the evidence of all of her things there, like she'd partially moved in with him.

Mother also loved going to her lodge, and she ate there a lot when there wasn't a new man keeping her away. Children at home just never registered as a responsibility for our mother.

Mother would come home and say, "You kids eat everything! And I'm sick of it! Lizzy, go to the store and get a loaf of bread. You all had better not touch it either!" Sometimes, by then, we were desperately needing to eat. We had to wait until she forgot about us again in order to go in and put peanut butter on bread.

My third grade year, Mother didn't fill out my free lunch slip, and I had no lunch ticket. I tried to tell her that I didn't have a lunch ticket early in the year, but she didn't want to give me money.

I made peanut butter sandwiches until the bread ran out. "You're using all of the bread, why do you eat so much? All you kids ever do is eat me out of house and home. Next time I get bread, you better leave it alone!" It was always a confusion in my life. How do I eat?

To keep out of her bread, I started putting fruit from cans in plastic sandwich bags, but the fruit cans in the pantry were limited. When I went to school, everyone made fun of me for my doubled up plastic sandwich bags full of canned fruit. I acted like this was my favorite meal and like nothing was wrong.

An intern sat with me one day, a young, negative lady. "Does your mother make that lunch for you, Lizzy?" She asked me this as she was looking with disdain at my dripping peach bag.

"No, I do," I had a smile that said it was a great lunch.

"Why fruit? Do you have other things at home you could bring?"

"No, but I like fruit, it's my favorite," I tried to say everything brightly.

She just sort of went about her lunch. She was tall, with short curly hair, and a pinched expression. I've met many people like her in my life: the people who look at you with great pity for your circumstances, while thinking somehow you are less than they are if this sort of thing happens to you. All the church gossips acted this way.

"Where is all of my fruit, goddamn it!?" Mother screamed at the top of her lungs. "I can't even come home and make a cobbler, you've eaten everything! Get in here, Lizzy!"

I hated being called in about food. "Did you eat all the canned fruit?" She would glare down at me in disgust.

"Yes, ma'am," I would say, as softly as a whisper.

"I'm going to buy more this afternoon, and you had better not touch it!"

"Yes, ma'am," I would whisper again, and stand stock still, until I felt I could walk away from her.

After she discovered I was eating her canned fruit, and bread was scarce, fruit was not an option. Most days that year I just went to school and didn't eat that day. I have known what hunger feels like. It was hard to sit around the school lunch table and watch all the other kids eat. The other kids always asked with sneers, "Why didn't you bring any lunch today, Lizzy?"

I just smiled a brilliant smile. "Oh, I just don't get hungry during the day," I announced. They all went back to their lunch.

MY FOUR

BROTHERS

1

JESSIE

Many mornings I wake up to a sky, to a smell in the air, that reminds me of Jessie. Until I was seven or eight years old, Jessie was my life. He was all that I had, but he didn't know or understand or want to be all that I had. Jessie was a boy, a young boy who was just trying to survive like I was. Maybe, now, I should forgive him too, for leaving my life, for not knowing how to love me, but the hardest part of letting this loss go is that I wanted for forever the love that he gave to me.

Jessie was different for me. I held on to him with all my might. I spent years confused by his silence towards me, but now I know, I understand. It's okay even. Our relationship was meant for the time that it was in and that was all. I can accept that. I know I can.

As I wander the world alone, not having built a life because I didn't know how to, I will always think of Jessie, and how in the purity of childhood, he was the only one who ever truly knew how to take care of me.

Yes, yes, I know…, it really wasn't his job.

"Jessie, Jessie, can I come in?" My voice at six was whispery and trembly. His room was Aunt May's room when she was gone.

"No, Lizzy, go to bed before Mama finds out you're awake." A surge of fear ran through me as I peeked into the room where Jessie slept. I was on my tiptoes holding onto the gold door knob with both hands.

"Please, can I come in for a little while?" The house was so cold that Jessie was sleeping on the floor with a blanket around him over the floor vent for heat when it came on. He always slept that way, winter and summer.

"No, go back to bed now, Lizzy. I don't want you in here, and

Mama's gonna whip you if she finds you here in the morning!" His voice was harsh, though still in a whisper.

"Please, we don't have to tell her. I'll wake up before she does and go to my room." I held onto the door knob, not thinking about what was behind my back in the hall. It was too much for me to think about. My ruffled, elasticy gown sleeves were cutting into my upper arms.

"No Lizzy, go to bed." His voice was always so harsh and distant.

"Please!" I squealed a little.

"What are you afraid of, Lizzy?" I heard the slight breakdown in his voice. I was changing his mind, and I knew it.

"I don't know. I don't know why I'm scared."

"Well, no one's going to get you, Lizzy," he lied. His voice was softer but still with a hint of harshness. He had pulled the cover back from his head to look at me for the first time.

"I don't know what I'm afraid of," I said again.

"Fine, but get up on the bed and let me sleep. Mama's going to whip you in the morning."

I sighed. I knew I still had to persuade his ten year old heart to let me sleep next to him on the floor. I was afraid of the windows the bed was beneath. I could see, in the small room, with Jessie at my feet at the end of the double bed, the broad monstrous moonlit windows. "Please let me sleep on the floor with you? I don't need to be under your heat tent. Can I just lie next to you?"

"No, Lizzy. I can't sleep with you right up against me. Sleep in the bed or go back to your room." His voice was harsh again and he covered his dark head quickly, letting me know that the conversation was over.

I stepped small feet around him and shut the door behind me. "Jessie, please can I sleep with you on the floor?"

"God, Lizzy, you drive me crazy. Fine, just get your own cover. You're not getting under mine." He turned his face toward the mahogany footboard in the too small room. The rest of the room was just a shadowy place in the moonlight. Not much fit in the room more than a bed, dresser, a TV, and my Aunt May's little cat table. She had collected cat statues. Jessie had put it in the closet for his stay in her room.

I grabbed a blanket from the bed, threw it on the floor with a pillow, and nestled myself against Jessie. He didn't move. I wondered if he was already asleep. He slept very hard. I hardly slept at all. I was too afraid to sleep. I was too aware of being alive for sleep.

I lay there staring at the ceiling when the covers that were loosely covering up Jessie flew up into a bubbled tent. He turned just long enough to open the side of his blanket to let me in. I didn't say a word. I just nestled in next to Jessie.

I spent countless nights in this ritual with Jessie. Sometimes I would wake him up just to be with me. It made him mad, but he always seemed to soften to me eventually.

"I'm afraid of dying." We lay under the cold, empty moonlit windows, in Aunt May's double bed.

"Lizzy, you woke me up for that? We all have to die, just don't think about it!" I hated the harshness of his voice.

"Are you afraid too?" I would ask while in the deepest concentration.

"I just don't think about it." After ten minutes maybe, his voice would soften. He knew, but at which point he knew is beyond me, that something was terribly wrong with me.

"I can't get free from thinking about it," I would say.

"Well, you have to, Lizzy, you just have to," and he would roll over and go to sleep on that particular subject.

Now, I know that many children have obsessive fears about death at certain stages. There's no great mystery in this fear. It's when the stage goes whack, and every stage of development goes whack along with it, that there's a problem.

"Lizzy, what are you doing?" Jessie stood at the hall entrance late in the night. I could see him mostly in shadow.

I realized I must have been dancing in the moonlit living room again, deep in the night, daring myself.

"I don't know, Jessie," I said. I paused in confusion with the moonlight flooding my body like a spotlight. "I don't know," I repeated, and I didn't really know. I hugged myself, shuddering instinctively.

"You're afraid of the dark, Lizzy!" He was puzzled, coming toward me. "Why are you out here in the middle of the night?"

"I don't know," I just said it over and over again. I felt scared and brought back to my normal ways of feeling scared. "Can I sleep with you?"

"Yes, but be quiet. I don't want to wake Mama up."

We went to Jessie's room. We didn't talk about things like that after they happened. I guess some of my behaviors were too much for children to sort out. We just went on with our lives like they didn't happen.

Jessie carried me through the early years. He knew something was wrong with me before I did.

When he stopped talking to me, I had a hard time recovering.

He didn't speak to me for eighteen years.

2

THE JESSIE-ELIZABETH

My family has reported that Jessie was seriously jealous of me after my adoption; he'd had our father all to himself for however long before I came into the picture. They say Jessie was also upset by starting kindergarten and having to leave our father during the day. Dad was a policeman and with his nighttime work schedule and Mother working during the day, he was the natural caregiver.

Dad owned a boat and took us out on the ocean on a regular basis or just took us drifting through local channels. The cabin wasn't always our destination. We lived very near the coast, and my father was a regular at local marinas.

My father named his boat after Jessie and myself. Our names stood out in huge, bold, stickered letters on the back of his Browning. He combined our names with a hyphen. I can't express to you what it was like as a child to hesitate, look down, and pretend not to see the back of the boat, when realizing that our names weren't on the back of the boat anymore, but that the name of his latest wife had taken our places.

I remember studying it, the back of the Browning, when no one was around. I went up, stood on a bucket and traced over our names that were still stained whiter than the actual white of the boat. Joy's name was short and mean. Ours was long enough together to still be seen on the outer edges of hers.

I don't remember having any emotion about the changing of the names on the boat; it's just a snapshot in my head of my past responses to things.

Jessie saw me, and shook his fist in rage, "Get away from there, get down, he doesn't love us anymore, no one loves us, no one ever will. Don't you know that? You're stupid, stop doing that. I can't stand you." He stomped off. His face was red, his eyes full of water. What was that water in his eyes? How did he do that?

I quietly slipped off my bucket, put it away, and steadily looked over the yard of my father's new home. Life was in pictures for me, panoramic snapshots that would come back in my dreams for the rest of my life. I knew that I was supposed to carry these images around with me forever. I just didn't know why. The sun was high. I had translucent hands. Nothing felt could ever be better than the world I lived in, the feeling of being untouchable by pain, being able to remove myself.

A little later I went to find Jessie, but he refused to play with me. He was a chunky eight year old who often shoved me away when he was angry. I always forgave him, though, just like he always forgave me. We were all hurting in inexplicable ways.

Jessie lost his natural father when he was two and a half years old. Out of her nine husbands, our mother made Jessie's father the saint. I don't know what to make of that, making people saints after death. It's confusing for me. I do know that she said that Jessie would wait at the door every day at four o'clock for the man, his birth father, to come home from work and play with him.

I wouldn't know anything about the kinds of feelings that Jessie had for his father. I was born to a teenage mother who didn't know who my father was. My birth mother said my birth father could have been one of two men. It doesn't matter to me now. There are so many other things that matter to me now, that I can hardly wince at the silly mistakes of an irrevocably damaged girl.

3

THE WOODS

Just so there's no confusion, in early childhood, the years after Dad left, I didn't *not* love my life. I didn't know any other way that my life could be, so I didn't really dwell on life with any kind of sad perspective. I don't believe I was sad. I wasn't pining away for love or affection I didn't get. I think we try to figure out our paths and missteps in adulthood. As a child I grabbed happiness where I could, and learned to cope with the rest.

Some of the best times in my life were after my father left; they were spent with Jessie for the first few years. I think that there was a good long while where no one really noticed Jessie and myself, so we were more free than we had been.

Jessie took me miles through the woods beyond the sand dunes. I was six and he was nine. He took me fishing and swimming. We built new worlds with forts in the tallest pine trees. We always had to nail wooden ladder steps up the pine trees because their limbs didn't usually grow all the way down their trunks.

Our trips always started like this: "You can't go with me, Lizzy!"

"Why not?" I would whine, barefoot, in raggedy jeans, in one of his old flannel shirts that no longer fit him. I was almost ready to go!

"Because, I'm just not taking you this time, you'll get tired of walking. You'll be noisy and scare the fish. No!" His face was stern, and his cheeks were red. The gray half zipped jacket wasn't doing much for him, but I don't think we felt the cold back then.

I squealed, "I never get tired of walking, you know that!"

"Aunt May's not going to let you go, anyway."

"She's asleep. She'll never know we left until we're gone." Aunt

May, who lived with us part time to help out with the kids, seemed to try and pin me down more than the boys.

"No, Lizzy, you can't go, and that's final!"

"But why? I can help carry your fishing gear." I was desperately trying to be convincing.

My feet felt like ice on Mother's huge concrete porch. The sun was so brilliant in the sky overlooking our street, that the feel, the smells, the light quality, took my breath away. Sometimes as an adult I see the sky that way, first thing in the morning, and it just stops me and keeps me standing still. It always makes me think of Jessie, our street, our time and place in the world. The feeling fills me up.

I waited patiently in the freezing cold for Jessie to finally give in. He always gave in eventually, without fail.

"Okay, but you have to carry the tackle bucket, the poles, everything, and you can't complain once, or you're not coming again!" His voice was sharp and serious. He was always serious.

I didn't even let him finish before I bolted for the door to get my shoes. I saw in his face that he was waiting for *what was in it for him* in taking me along. He always let me go, but he always made me beg first. This was the game we played. Jessie always had to have power over whatever we were doing. I think it might be a big brother, little sister thing.

We covered miles under pine trees, watching dump trucks as we trudged through the sand dunes to reach those trees. I loved the smell of the world, when I could still smell it. When I remembered that, that was what was important. I remembered to love just being alive.

"Be quieter, Lizzy. Don't rattle so much. That old man doesn't like us going through his yard."

"Okay," I would whisper, with my jacket now tied around my waist. The gear was heavy and I was hot. "How much longer until we're there?"

"Don't ask me that, you said you weren't going to complain!"

"I just wanted to know how much further," I started.

"Shhhh. . ."

"Fine," I trudged until the end of the world, and felt the tired muscles in my arms. I loved following Jessie, no matter where that road led.

We could be building a fort together:

"Lizzy, you have to find boards that are this size. Those are too small." "Such a useless girl," he would mumble under his breath, but I felt loved just the same.

"You have to use two nails or else the ladder will just be spinning everywhere!" He demonstrated the spinning step on the trunk of the tree. His dark hair just bounced, it was so heavy and thick. He was staring at the trunk of the tree. I was staring at it, too, with brilliant, wild, dark, alive eyes.

"Humph," I mouthed as I went for the next nail. "Well, we're gonna need to find more nails then."

I was so completely enthralled in what we were doing. I didn't even want to stop to go home for the bathroom. I just found a place to squat in the woods. I remember squatting in hidden shrubs, and looking up to the heaven of tree tops. The glistening sun was my friend. Life was so beautiful. I didn't know why I felt so good, or why I seemed to feel life coursing through me. I was overwhelmed by existence. Maybe it was the contrast of the complex pain and melancholy of most events against the awe of life experienced without pain.

Sometimes when we went swimming in the summer time, one of Jessie's friends would tag along, which made it extra hard for me to get to go. I had to beg harder, or give him something that I loved.

The pond we went to we called "Rakes Pond." It was surrounded by a rich forest all the way around it to its edges; we played at the lake's only opening.

We had ropes hanging from the opening trees, and I can't tell you how marvelous it was to stare out over this huge lake and watch the sun splash across it. I had this sense of awe at the magnificence of it. The sounds of the birds and water life were so alive. I knew, somehow, that the lake and the natural world in general were so old, and that I was only a blink to them. I felt like the trees knew that I was just a visitor to a world where they were the elders, where they were the gods of reality. I felt that they could love me and that I could love them. We were free to do that.

There was one gnarled tree on the water that the boys could climb way up into its branches and use its heaviest branch as a diving board. I don't know how high it was, but I was afraid of it. When I was brave enough to climb up to the diving branch and look down without jumping, it seemed like I was standing on the top of a house.

I would climb up and look down, but I could not jump, until Jessie noticed that I didn't jump and started taunting me about it. I never wanted Jessie to think I couldn't do anything he was doing.

"Jump, Lizzy! Don't be a chicken!" Jessie shouted. "Jump to the shallow part and I'll make sure you can touch."

I said nothing, standing on the branch with my hands wrapped around an upper branch for support. I was swimming in old black shorts and a black t-shirt. I remember having knobby knees.

"Jump, Lizzy! You're such a baby, jump already, you're not going to die, for God's sake!"

I stared down into the murky brown water. His voice seemed like an echo from another time and place. I had to do it now, I thought, but I didn't know how to do it. Jessie's fragile framed friend Darrin was sitting next to me on the branch. He was a crude, disgusting mouthed boy, but not a mean, bullying boy, so he didn't really say anything.

"If you don't jump, I'm not bringing you back with me! I can't stand you being a baby!"

My mind was gravely ignoring of Jessie. I knew what Jessie was saying, thinking, and threatening. This was common in our dynamic. I knew I had to jump. I was just figuring out how to face that fact as I stood above the water. How could I make myself do it? Nothing was going to separate me from Jessie.

Finally I sat down at the farthest edge of the limb. My wet black shirt was drying. My hands were clamped to the branch.

"Darrin, I need you to push me off the limb!"

"What?" He looked stunned, while Jessie sang out below some song he'd made up about my being a chicken.

"I need you to push me, when I'm not paying attention." My toes dangled so far in the air that it made me queasy.

His eyes bulged, and a half smile formed, "Are you sure, Lizzy?"

"Yes, I'll turn away and you just push! Okay!" My heart started to race.

I looked away for not even a second when I felt the falling sensation. I just went to another world. When I felt the splat and splash, and when I felt my feet on dirt, I was so genuinely jazzed to still be living. I was also thrilled with myself to high heaven. Jessie was clambering to make sure I reached the shallow part, because

I never learned to swim, and Darrin was laughing so hard he was trembling.

Jessie just told me, "See, I told you it was nothing. You can't be afraid of things like that."

Darrin came down and told Jessie what had happened, and told me how neat he thought it was that I was so brave. I was glowing with pride.

Jessie just laughed at Darrin's story about how I'd made him push me, not really acknowledging me, but I knew he was proud too, in his own way.

Mine and Jessie's lives, for a few years, were just like that: From Cowboys and Indians, where I always had to be the Indian no matter what or he wouldn't let me play; to board games where he always had to be black in checkers. I forget which piece he had to be in Monopoly, but there was a specific piece.

There was also the endless building of bike ramps that I shouldn't have taken a ten speed over at seven; the bike was too big for me. But, as you can imagine, the boys were awful proud of my flips as I miraculously came up without a scratch. It was a glorious life.

"Jessie, just let me go. Don't make me stay at home," I can hear my own little voice now, and it changes the images I had of myself. It changes my avoidance of remembering myself at all in my life as Lizzy.

I think, as I'm writing this, I'm learning to like her, Lizzy, not to avoid her, not to deny her, not to be hurt by having been her, that girl I used to be. She was okay, funny even, as she manipulated herself into the arena of something good.

"Good for you, Lizzy, good for you! And..., God bless your brother, Jessie," I say to myself now, since no one ever said it to me in those days, when Jessie let me go into the natural world, trailing along behind him.

"Good for you, Lizzy, good for you."

4

THE DREAM

Mr. Revel lived across the street. When I was a little girl, he was very nice to me. He stood in the carport of a simply designed house. He had a porch that was windowed in; the porch ran along the full length of the front of his house. For some reason, his front porch stars in many of my odd "movie reel" dreams, along with his backyard fence which overlooked cliffs of sand dunes.

His front yard was a garden of fenced in green and when you raised your eyes you met the meticulously made windows. Each window was a column of small rectangular pieces of glass. If your eyes went to the right, you would see Mr. Revel's cement driveway that led up to the carport where he always stood. He would smoke, hiding that fact from his wife, and hiding from her, his wife, in general, though I know he loved her.

I was confused by Mr. Revel being home all the time, even though to me he was old as old could be. I wondered why he didn't work. At some point he explained to me that he had to retire from a delivery company early because he had a serious heart defect and his doctor wouldn't allow him to work anymore. He always explained everything to me when we talked; he was very clear. I remember liking standing with him, being recognized, not invisible. When I saw Mr. Revel, I would suddenly feel awake to life for a moment and run and say hello.

"Hey there, Lizzy. What are you doing with this fine and beautiful day?"

"Oh, nothing much. What are you doing?"

"Well, my son's coming over to show me his new truck today. He bought a new truck this past weekend." All of his children were grown and one of his daughters lived next door to him in a tan doublewide trailer. She still lives there to this day.

Mr. Revel had a brilliant smile. He grabbed for his smokes which were hidden in his front jacket pocket. He winked at me. "Don't tell Martha, now."

"Oh no, I won't." I felt my face brighten in a smile. I would then run off and do whatever was my next plan for the day.

Mr. Revel's driveway was also our elementary school bus stop for some years in the later part of my elementary school experience, and he was outside every morning to say "good morning" to all of us, the straggly neighborhood kids. He called me his Lizzy Brat after my father was gone. I may have even been grateful to him for that. I must have missed my father, though I don't remember feeling the missing. It's more like a broken nagging piece of yourself way deep inside that's there but you just don't think about it on the surface anymore.

I have a couple of dreams about Mr. Revel's house, about his yard. He's not in them, and his wife is not in them either. Here is one of those dreams.

In this particular dream I'm six years old and standing on the dirt road that lines the back yards of that row of homes on Mr. Revel's side of the street. The sand dunes that usually had dump trucks coming in and out of the pits to gather dirt at various times of the day are unnervingly quiet. There are no trucks, no human life, on this day, in this dream. The sky grows darker every moment. We, Jessie and I, are losing daylight at a rapid pace. It's like someone is controlling a dimmer switch, and watching us.

Jessie, who is nine, is pacing. He is agitated, upset, and going to be angry and cry. I just know he is going to cry. He is so frustrated with being alive. Living hurts him so much. I am nervous, too, in the dream. Mr. Revel's gate is locked and we won't be able to cut through his yard to get home. The dark forest that surrounds the dunes is calling us home to oblivion, to some place where everything goes black, because a day in our lives has just such an unbearable feeling.

As Jessie and I stand in front of the gate, suddenly an old, black, broken down car appears before us in Mr. Revel's back yard.

Jessie screams at me, "Take off your clothes and get in the car or go with me now! But I'm leaving, Lizzy, I'm leaving!" He's panicked, bewildered, angry; he doesn't want to know about his aloneness in the world. His tears are falling. He's pacing so hard that he's stomping prints into the heavy dirt beneath his feet. His hands are grabbing at the gate that's now suddenly wide open to this dark, black car.

Jessie paces by nature, he's always done that, so his fear is not what is making me afraid. My brain is watching, scoping out the constantly changing images. I'm agitated, I'm nervous like an addict. I don't feel fear like Jessie is feeling. My muscles just tighten in my animal way.

Jessie's hands fly in the air with a last desperate attempt to get me to join him as he runs from what is to come. "I mean it, Lizzy. Make a choice, make it now, I'm leaving! Take off your clothes, get in the car, or go with me!"

I scan his tear-stained face and his trembling chin just before he disappears. He needs a haircut. His hair is so thick and dark. Jessie and I have the same eyes. Looking into Jessie's eyes to this day is like looking into a mirror of my own.

Jessie is gone. The car gets darker, more sinister. My stomach turns. The night has come.

I run to the left of the car, but I can't get away. I grab the fence, because the more I try to run, the more I get sucked backwards in slow motion. I can see my house. No lights are on. I strain, tearing at the fence. I try to get away from the car. I can see my fingers pulling at the chainlink fence, trying to gain ground over what lies behind and beside me. I can no longer move my feet to try and run.

The world goes black.

The world is sometimes full of darkness. I wonder why that is, but I've never truly minded the darkness part.

Even as a small child, I preferred nothingness over fear. Fear is worse than death.

5

QUENTIN

Although my sister, Leslie, was our mother's late life caregiver, Quentin was our mother's life. Quentin is who our mother called several times a day, for no apparent reason, and the one she called at three in the morning on the nights she believed she would go insane.

Quentin fully sacrificed his life for our mother, and I wish she had thought more about what she had done to him, but she didn't. Mother loved Quentin, but not as much as he loved her. Quentin was real, and Mother was not capable of being real. Mother could never think beyond herself.

Quentin always gave everything of himself to take care of other people, especially our mother. Quentin didn't have much time, in my mind, to take care of a bride and children, when his life was tied up with Mother. He lived around the block from our mother and came by several times a day to check in on her. This is just what Quentin had always done.

Quentin's marriage didn't work out, but none of us six siblings had relationships that worked out. We didn't have models that made us believe or be enthusiastic about the idea of forever. We weren't cynical people. We all tried to have positive relationships that would last, but we could only allow people to get so close to us. We all had a secret that no one could know, and we were all taught that we were valueless. When anyone got close enough to us to see that we believed that way about ourselves, we turned on them, to prove to that person that we were, in fact, valueless.

Quentin was the shadow in my life, as long as I could remember. He, many times, took Mother's attention away from me, redirected her. But sometimes he didn't redirect her.

"Stay out of her way, Lizzy!" His dark eyes would look into me earnestly. "Stay out of her way as much as you can!" It was like Quentin saw her dam breaking, accepted this as our life, and he just did what he could, when he could.

Quentin was good to me. We didn't share the same life beliefs, later, as a whole, but one fundamental belief we did share: we were us, and we would always be, forever and ever. It's like we siblings are the club. We, each of us, have the same look in our eyes. We are the only ones that get each other, or understand the depth of what our experience has been. We are only safe to be ourselves when we are together.

I think about Quentin's smile, when I picture him. His smile was a monumental occurrence. It was contagious and real. His smile was always the key to his soul for me; it was always the thing that made me feel he was so courageous. If Quentin could accept the reality of our lives, and still smile, then he was really something.

In my early adult years, I heard it over and over again from Quentin, who was, as always, trying to solve the unsolvable problem of Mother's unhappiness: "Lizzy, come see her. This is wrong, what you're doing!" His voice was reasonable.

"I can't, I'm sorry! I can't come home!"

"You have to be loyal to your family, Lizzy. We're all we have!"

"Yes, yes, I know you must be right, but no, I can't, not right now!"

"Lizzy, what if she dies tomorrow, she may not have much time left, I don't want you to regret your choice to stay away. I don't care about her, I'm thinking of you!"

"I'm not coming home!"

"Okay, but I really hope you don't regret this!" I could hear the sigh, and the defeated sound in his voice.

And then, after years of asking me to come home, I think he finally understood that it didn't make sense, because..., well..., because, it didn't make sense. What was I going home to? And Quentin was a stronger person than me.

I'd spent my life trying to keep my mind safe. It was slow and methodical work for me. My keeping my mind safe was never a choice. I am a dissociative person, a person in many parts. My selves kept myself away, when I could not.

6

BRENT

I don't intend to write about my brother, Brent, and the sexual abuse that occurred. I was in the boy's back room when he got into the bed with me for the first time. He told me what to do, and I just did it. That's what I was taught to do. I didn't act in a way, I guess, that showed my disgust, or the sick feelings I carried with me, on a daily basis.

I don't intend to write about Brent, because I believe Brent may have been a victim, too. I believe my brother was taught his behavior towards me. So, it wouldn't be right for me to go against a brother that I dearly love. That's that, and there is nothing else about it for me that I want to live within. I'll take him with me, through eternity, with love for him that's intact, unconquerable, and alive.

My disassociation did not come from Brent, and Brent ran away as the very worst parts of my life began.

When I knew Brent later in my life, when I was fourteen years old, I was told I had to go to my sister's to babysit for her for the night. I hadn't seen him in maybe six years. Leslie would be out all night, bartending, and I'd heard before I was to go over to her house that Brent, who was then a young adult, was staying with her for a while.

I felt hysterical inside, at the thought of running into Brent. There was no one I could tell about it either, so I had to go, and I had to hope that I could protect myself.

In my sister's trailer, I played with my infant niece, while I waited for my sister to leave for work. She kept asking me what was wrong. I hadn't said very much. I just told her I wasn't feeling well.

When the door knob turned and Brent came into the room, he was glad to see me. He grabbed me, hugged me. I can't put into words what was going on in my head, the fear and panic that I was trying to hide. I looked like an untraceable empty person.

Brent looked the same as he did in childhood, only taller, and older. He was blonde, striking, but not pretty. He and Keith always had this charismatic, handsome quality about their appearances. I think this came from their father, the one our mother didn't like, and punished the two boys accordingly for it.

I was nervous, and I remember the nervousness was starting to come out in the agitation in my voice when I talked to Brent. Leslie was there, but quickly blew off my behaviors. She was used to me acting oddly and telling me to get a hold of myself. She'd always confronted me about my social anxiety, but could never grasp why it was so. She needed me to be like she was, laid back, letting it all go, and I wish I could have been that for her. It took me years to leave her for good, because I couldn't be what made her comfortable.

Brent never did anything to me again. He was happy to see me at Leslie's and loved me in an endearing and sweet way from then on out. He visited me even eventually at my own place on a regular basis. "Hey, Sis, how are you? Just stopped in to say hi." He was always welcome.

As we got older, the love of his life was Margret Ann. He had apparently been with this beautiful, waif-like young woman since he had run away from our mother's house. Margret Ann was sweet, beautiful, and even tinier than Leslie, because she was shorter, I suppose. She had these luminous, alive, dark eyes. Her auburn hair lay straight down her back. Brent lived with her and her father for many years.

Brent and Margret Ann started having trouble, and I didn't see him for a time. When he was with her and her father, he kept himself together, worked hard, that kind of thing, but without them, he took a terrible turn. I'd heard about it, from my other siblings at some point, but then he and Margret Ann started breaking up and getting back together a lot, so I heard about it from him, too. I saw the differences in him when they were together and when they were apart. When they were together, he'd stop by in his happy go lucky way, and when they were apart, he just didn't come around.

Finally, the two, Margret Ann and Brent, who were together most of their lives, had split for their longest period of time yet, and

Margret Ann was living with someone else. I didn't see Brent much anymore, and when I ran into him he was lost, living a partially out of control life, but still holding on in some capacity, maybe.

Margret Ann had died. She was epileptic and had a seizure while taking a bath and drowned. Brent came to me after she died, just to talk, and he did seem to still be somewhat together.

"I never let her take baths alone. You're not supposed to let her take a bath alone." His voice was fumbly, far away.

"Yes, I didn't know, I'm sorry."

"I can't believe he didn't take care of her. Can you believe he didn't take care of her?"

"No, no, I can't." My voice felt so small. He looked drained, world weary, too far traveled.

"I wish that I'd been there. This never would have happened if I'd been there." Soft wetness escaped his eyes. He wouldn't look at me directly.

"I know. I wish you'd been there, too."

"I loved her; I never would've let that happen to her. You had to watch her."

"I know, I know."

"Many times I had helped her with her seizures. I knew what to do."

"I'm so sorry, honey, I'm so sorry," I whispered as he went on in his own head, in his own way.

But sorry would never be enough, nothing would ever be enough. His light went out. Margret Ann was the only love he'd ever known or could understand, in this life. He was moderately fine with her living, and the possibility of reconciliation, but her death proved to be the end of him. He was never the same again. He seemed to always have something with a different vulnerable woman who he wouldn't stay with in the end. He would get strung out, from what I was told was drugs and alcohol, but I didn't see the drugs. I only saw the alcohol. We would all slowly lose contact with him for years at a time.

I did see Brent again, maybe seven years ago. He was in a hospital in Georgia having some kind of heart issue. He had ruined his health with his hard lifestyle. Leslie and I drove up together, to see that he was okay. Brent was nothing of what he was before. He was flip, not real, you name it. I never really wanted to know him after that. I knew my brother Brent had died with Margret Ann. I let it go at that.

I'm sorry for Brent's sweetness lost. All of my brothers' hearts, from the start, were, honestly, everything that was good. Our mother had very good men for sons. I wish she had known how to nurture that.

7

KEITH

In Mother's doublewide, her room took one end of it, with two other bedrooms and a bathroom along a hall. At the start of the hall, there was a dividing wall between the living room and the kitchen. So you had a choice when standing at the head of the hall: you could go into the living room that stretched to the other end of the trailer, or you could step left into the kitchen that split three quarters of the way down into the dining area.

There was no wall dividing the living room and dining area. If you went into the kitchen, there was no longer a back door; the old back door went into an addition that was built on for the four boys. First you stepped into the laundry area that was very small and led to an actual new back door. But the other door in the brown paneling board laundry room went to the boy's big back room; the boy's room went the rest of the length of the trailer.

I don't know what I remember about the boy's room before our father left, but I do remember a scene when he had just gone. Because my mother never fell into my mind before my father left, there was one image of her that has stayed with me. I was holding a doll, I think, standing in that backroom doorway. Mother was holding a broom while straddling my brother, Keith, who was also holding the broom, trying to keep it off his neck.

I remember freezing there, inappropriately staring at both of them straining to have control over the broom. Both of them had red faces and the veins in their necks were bulging. My mother's voice was shallow from the strain.

"I'll kill you," she seethed. "I'll kill you and I'll get away with it too!"

I don't remember much else, and maybe I have the words wrong.

Only Keith would really know, and maybe Jessie or Brent, who at that time were watching in horror, maybe.

I actually don't remember engaging at any point with Keith, my second to the oldest brother, before this new knowledge of his protecting himself from my mother was frozen in my brain. It's funny sometimes how the world takes shape before us. Looking back now, it feels like the world in my mind was like a lilting petal in the wind, not quite real or tangible, everything was questionable…, and then, suddenly, the world became absolute and concrete. What wasn't extinguishable was suddenly inescapable and present. I didn't like being present. It was exhausting and scary for me.

I don't know much about the war between my mother and Keith. I know that Keith spent time in a boy's home for misbehavior after Dad left. Maybe he stole stuff, maybe he acted out, I don't remember really, or maybe I don't choose to remember, or maybe I just don't care one way or the other. He was kind to me when I would learn to know him in later years.

There was a family story that my mother used to tell with a shameful pride. She said that she was on our concrete front porch with Keith and maybe three other adults when she shoved Keith to the ground. Keith hurt his arm, was violently upset, and screaming that he would call some kind of Child Services.

My mother proudly noted whenever she would retell this story that the adults around her just told him, "Boy, I saw you fall down. Child Services aren't going to do anything for you!"

Mother said all of this my whole life, so proudly. She had never treated Keith or Brent, the middle boys, the way she treated Jessie and Quentin. She made her feelings for the boys openly known.

Mother made a distinction, decided the worth, of two boys that ached for her love their entire lives. She told them they were worthless, and they believed it, and one completely self destructed. She told us all we were worthless though, at different times. With Keith and Brent, and myself, there was such a complete lack of control in the way she hurt us, or the way she took her life out on us. I'll always wonder what demon she was trying to put to death on our broken bodies.

After Dad went away, Leslie was with him a majority of the time. Keith left for whereever. Quentin got married at seventeen or eighteen, to the girl around the block. Brent, Jessie, and myself, we all just dangled in the wind, watching the destruction.

The first image I have of Keith in memory, other than the group of us on the river, which remains elusive and dreamy, is of my mother straddling him, a son that she could not bring herself to love. Her face was red, her body was massive. She was a living monster. But I will love Keith, and I will love all of us. I will love us so much that all of the unloving mothers in the world will feel ashamed.

THE MOTHER

1

THE MOTHER

I had a romantic attachment to the sky, the way it looked just before the sun took over. It was like me, that early light, I just knew it. I would never be brazen like the sun.

Things ran together for me in my first early years, things like color, bright and dark light, smells, different feelings and behaviors from other humans, and actual textures, too.

I collected information in my head. I collected lines from conversations. I collected the direction of the wind as it caressed my face in different seasons. I even collected in my mind the way that, when I marched across my bed to get to the window to peep out, my feet would sink into the mattress, just so. Everything was filling up a memory bank inside of me.

I know that I started compiling this memory bank because I lost them, my siblings. I know the bank was needed because I didn't pay attention when I had my sister and my brothers. I was the biggest fool at four for not retaining every second of the time that I knew them. I have such regret about that. Why didn't I understand that no amount of remembering after they were gone from my life would ever bring them back again?

My first memory of the Mother was to just simply wonder about her. I don't know that I was so afraid of her then, as I would learn to be in later years, and then, did I fear her later? I just don't know. Existing where the Mother was would simply be about survival instincts, I guess, because I'm not sure if I would know that her future attacks would be undeserved. How could I know that? Why would a person be afraid of what was justice?

The way she was with the doctors confused me, talking to them in a false way that made me want to vanish into a world without consciousness.

The Mother's energy always vibrated like an earthquake. I couldn't help but get lost in the trembling. I was molded to the only life that I knew.

My mother was the black night that innocence stepped into. Innocent people wanted whatever it was that Mother had, that made them drawn to her, but then, after knowing her, and watching her blackness, they would never be the same again.

2

THE FLOATING GRANDMOTHER

"She was floating, floating like she was lying in her casket! Her hair was hanging silver, gray! I saw her! I saw her! I was awake, sitting up in bed, watching her float around my room!" Silence followed this exclamation.

"Quentin, Quentin, are you listening to me? She was wearing the blue floral dress I picked out for her burial. It didn't even hang down like her hair did. It was like the coffin pillows were invisible underneath the dress part of her as she floated. Her hands were still folded across her chest." I listened to the half panic in her voice.

The Mother was grabbing at her own massive arms. The smoke from her cigarette hung thickly around her and filled the dining room. She was in one of her greenish, blue gowns. For me, she was just coming into focus as another human being that lived around me.

My body felt frail as I stumbled from bed to get a drink of water.

I'd never had to be aware of my frailness until this time in my life, when she came into it fully, the time that I would learn to know her. I felt trembly inside.

"Quentin, I don't know what to do," she wailed. Her hair was matted with sweat. "I can't go back to sleep. I know she'll come again!" The Mother didn't really make eye contact with Quentin, who stood at the end of the table in his blue work clothes. The Mother couldn't remain focused.

I hid behind her big living room chair, trying not to be noticed. I quietly kneeled down, instinctively knowing not to be visible, not to move, not to go back to my room, and not to move to go forward.

"Mama, stop it, it was just a dream!" Quentin seemed unnerved by her. He always did. Apparently, I was just learning, everybody always felt unnerved by her.

"She's trying to hurt me," the Mother wailed, grabbing at her arms again. "I knew she hated me! I knew she'd never leave me alone. " The Mother was frantic for some kind of comfort, or maybe she wasn't. Maybe she wanted attention.

"Mama, Grandma is not trying to hurt you, it was a bad dream! You've got to pull it together!" He looked disgusted.

"She blamed me for her terrible life. She hated me." The Mother moved to wringing her hands rather than her arms. I could see her clearly.

"I don't know anything about that, Mama, but she's dead, she's gone!"

"She'll never be gone!" The slight frantic quality returned to her voice, but I still couldn't grasp the reality of what the Mother was doing. I noticed an open mayonnaise jar in front of her from the night before. She ate mayonnaise and never put it away until hours later. I don't think you're supposed to do that.

"As she lay in the hospital dying, she blamed me for her being there! She told me that I was the reason she lay there dying! There were tanks of blood beside the bed! I will never forget it!"

"What did you tell her?" my brother asked. "What did you tell her when she blamed you?"

The Mother started chanting, "She'll never be gone! She'll never be gone!" It was like Quentin hadn't even spoken to her.

"Mama, I'll check on you later tonight." That's all he could do. He lived around the corner. Quentin didn't get into the drama side of her; that was becoming clear. He just put up with her.

"You can't leave me like this!" Her eyes seemed to take on this enormous quality as she stared up at him.

"I have to work, Mama!" He pushed one hand through his thick dark hair, exasperated. He was in his blue buttoned down work shirt.

My knees were burning because I'd been kneeling down in the rough dark carpet for too long. I had to move myself, readjust. I accidentally bumped the wall behind the multicolored chair, just slightly, with the bottom of my foot. The Mother knew it was me instantly.

"Get her the hell out of here! I don't want her around me! Get out, go to your room!"

I saw her face turn into a person that was in a lot more control than the person that was sitting wringing her hands and clutching herself. This part was confusing. I wondered how a person could change so much, or have so many odd behaviors at once.

Every muscle in my fragile body always tensed when she put her attention on me, and they did in that moment. I was so tense that I didn't know how to run. I'd only wanted to ask if I could get some water when I came into the living room that morning to where she was. I couldn't go to the bathroom, hardly, without asking.

"Go to your room, Lizzy!" Quentin was firm, but he was never mean to me. He came up to me, seeing that I was caught in her wildness, and turned me toward the hall. I was grateful.

The living room was barely lit except for the breaking dawn and a lamplight on the bar in the dining room. When I was back in my room, I stood on my bed so that I could gaze out at the beginnings of the day. I got a splinter in my finger from the dark window frame that I held onto for balance.

3

HOME

When I felt the massive, muscular hand wrap around my forearm, I didn't know what was happening to me. I was nine. I didn't have time to think, and I don't know if it really seemed out of the ordinary to me to have that kind of experience—a sudden grabbing.

My arm was a child's arm. My body stiffened instinctively, as I was flung across my mother's living room floor. I felt my shoulder and the side of my head crash into the carpet. There was a burning feeling on the side of my face. I was bewildered, frantically trying to remember what she, (my mother), could have found out that I did. With my body sprawled and my head in the carpet, I couldn't remember anything, this time, that I had done.

My father had dropped me off after I had visited him for the weekend. He didn't walk me to the door of my mother's doublewide. He never did. He never wanted to be in the presence of my mother.

It was a beautiful sunny day as we pulled into the loneliest driveway in the world. I remembered wishing, but not allowing myself to truly wish, that I could have stayed with my father longer, or forever. I had an instinct inside, though. I knew that's not what he wanted. Being connected to me meant being more connected to her, and that's all there was to it. Although my father was telling me goodbye with some sense of sadness, he wasn't unhappy about getting back to his life. I don't know what I feel about that.

I was getting out of Dad's truck, which was always whatever the latest model was. I think this one was some kind of Ford. It was blue this time, with perfect interior; he was emphatic about keeping things up.

"Do you have everything?" Dad smiled, trying to keep his voice from sounding agitated. I knew he was worried that at any moment my mother would spring from the house.

"Yes, sir," I answered and slipped off the seat with one foot already on the paved drive.

"Call me if you need me, Lizzy," he said as he put the truck in gear.

"Yes, sir," I said again, though I knew he didn't mean it. For a moment he and I were both deeply submerged under the normal reality of my life.

I climbed the cinderblock steps like I always did, with nothing in particular going on in my head except the feeling I always felt upon being returned home. I just felt the pain of where I had to be. I think that abused children just live what they know how to live, accept it maybe. Like anything else, there were good days and bad days.

I pulled open the partial screendoor, unsuspecting. I held the screendoor open with my right hand, while trying to turn the knob and push the heavy, brown, interior door. My washed out pinkish bag was tossed over my shoulder. As I pushed the door, everything blurred.

Mother grabbed me and threw me across the living room carpet. Jessie sat in a big living room chair, watching.

"What did you tell him?" she screamed and snarled. I felt the whoosh of the heavy door being forced closed at a powerful rate. I didn't have time to answer her.

"What did you tell him?" She grabbed me off the floor, yanking me into the air. I felt like a rag doll. Her face was red, and sweat was pouring down her temples.

"Who?" I managed to stutter in the air. Mother couldn't hear me, though. She was gone into her own head. She started beating me with her free hand as she flung me around her living room. Jessie watched.

"I'm going to beat you until you tell me what you told him about me. You're a little bitch and I know you've been telling people about me." She was screaming so loud that I knew the neighbors were hearing.

I didn't say a word. She kept talking to herself, but directing it at me. I couldn't tell who the 'him' was but I was assuming she meant my father.

"I hate you! You're an ungrateful little bitch. You go and love your perfect father and then talk about me. He never did anything for you, but you adore him, it makes me sick." All this was coming as she was dangling me partially into the air, slapping at my head. I could barely use one foot for footing as she drug me.

Jessie watched it all, sitting in a living room chair.

I didn't dare cry while my mother beat me. That would have made it worse. I spent my time trying not to feel the blows, but the side of my head was starting to feel hollow and tingly, from the stinging.

I heard a beating on the door while my mother kept screaming, "So, what did you tell him? What did you tell him, you ungrateful little bitch?"

I then heard screaming at the door. "Susan, stop hitting her, stop hitting her, Jerry was drunk, he didn't think about what he was saying." It was my mother's best friend, Aunt Carol and her latest husband Jerry from next door.

"I'm going to kill her, and then she won't go talking to the neighbors about me." She was holding me in front of the window and slapping my face where Aunt Carol and Jerry could see. My hair was stuck around my wet rag doll face. Unfelt tears came naturally from, I guess, pure body release, because I wasn't in any kind of fear or panic anymore.

"Stop it, Susan, the child hasn't done anything. Jerry was just drunk. He didn't mean to say that you didn't feed her."

Mother just told them to go away, and they did. Jerry appeared to be in great despair over the situation. I don't think he knew a woman could do what my mother was doing, but they left all the same.

Mother picked up her belt and started beating me from the back of my calves to the front of my stomach, whatever she could get at. I finally wet my pants as she beat me; I couldn't hold anything in any more. She didn't even notice.

She just wailed even louder, "You told him I don't feed you, didn't you? I bet you spent the weekend telling your father that I don't feed you."

Jessie finally jumped up and screamed, "It's enough, you've got to stop, it's enough! She's wet her pants! You've got to stop! You can't kill her!"

"I can do any fucking thing that I want. I own her. I bet she doesn't tell anyone anything else about me," she snarled, with me in a wadded ball at her feet. She had exhausted herself.

I know it may seem strange, but my whole body felt numb lying there in a heap. The stinging was an odd sensation that mingled with the numb qualities. I just didn't feel so bad; I just didn't mind the blows. I don't think I processed them the way other people do. I just went away inside, buckled myself down somehow, and waited for it all to be over. Even in my adult life now, pain has to really knock me back. Before I feel it, the pain has to be extreme.

Mother sent me out of her sight, to my room. I got up, tired out and sweating. I used my body as I could, dragging myself down the hall.

"I can't stand you, you ruined my life, you little bitch! I shouldn't have ever adopted you!" she screamed after me, red faced and exhausted.

She should have had a heart attack. Then the future would have looked different. But I never thought those things as I survived, then. Then I would have rather stuck to the abuse that I knew, than be thrown into something new that might have been worse.

I just lay in my bed, and marveled at the stinging sensations.

I lay in a wounded body, staring at a white ceiling, and just vibrated with it all.

I didn't hate her, my mother; I didn't know her enough to hate her.

Jessie consoled her, I suppose, after I went to my room. She always had to be consoled after she beat me almost unconscious. That was the way of things. There were all these reasons why she had to do it, why she had to almost annihilate me.

I can't say that she beat me all the time in childhood, but it was an eggshell life I lived, wondering when she would. And she did, too many times.

I'd gone to dinner with the neighbors; my Aunt Carol had invited me. Her husband, Jerry, didn't like my mother or her treatment of me. While I was away at my dad's for the weekend, Jerry got drunk and told my mother that I ate like I'd not eaten in a long time. None of what I had been blamed for had anything to do with me. He just revved her up for what, at that time in our lives, seemed to be what she loved most to do.

4

THE CUPCAKES

When Mother came into my small bedroom, I could feel the warnings, and the different energy in her voice. Children of abuse learn to feel the weather of life's changes, like an animal that's smelling the coming rain. Even though I didn't know how to feel human feelings, I did learn to feel the different energies of all that was around me. My siblings and I, we were like little white rabbits, alert and trembling. Our people wisdom, our intuitions, became heightened. It's an eerie acknowledgement, small consolation, at best.

My siblings and I made a life of wondering *"What's going to happen next?"*, and after a while in that life, you're just in tune to the behaviors of people. I used to watch as someone new walked through my mother's door. I watched and waited for sounds in their voice and their use of language. I watched for behaviors, how someone might use their hands. It's hard to grasp maybe, unless you were children like us. We just honed skills that other people didn't use.

"Get your ass out of bed. I want to talk to you." I felt the wind of the door as she smashed it open. She always came with a crash or a wind sound at this time in our lives. She was trodding, and always heavy.

I got up, put on clothes and walked through the kitchen to where my mother waited in the dining room for me. Her mahogany dining table was turned long ways and pressed against the dining room window. Mother sat in the middle facing the window. Jessie sat at the end of the table that was open to the living room. I sat at the end of the table that was against the dining cabinets.

"I'm going to ask you something, and you better not lie to me."

She glared at me. My stomach dropped hollow, and my eyes had not yet focused clearly from sleep.

"Yes, ma'am." I sat at attention. My chair was not under the table but turned to face her.

"If you lie to me, I'm going to beat you unconscious!"

"Yes, ma'am." My stomach was rolling then.

"You took cupcakes from your Aunt Carol's house, and ate them."

"Aaron gave me a pack of cupcakes after school yesterday." Aaron was a temporary, almost adopted, son of my Aunt Carol's. He didn't live with her very long. I think he was a year younger than Jessie.

"He did not. Now you tell me the truth, or I'm going to beat you to death, but I'm going to beat you to death, anyway. You're a little bitch, and you make my life miserable." She edged her chair over to where she could be directly in front of me. The morning sun was shining into her face. There were, actually, rays beaming into the room.

"I didn't take the cupcakes! He gave me a pack of them!" I started to panic. My body was trembling in that animal way that it did when there was no release of pressure.

"You stole them, you're a liar!" she sneered.

I stopped trembling when her hand hit the side of my face. Her hands were muscular and long. The bottom of her hand hit my lips as the greater mass of her hand cupped over my ear that I'd had surgery on twice already.

My head went rigid. I just didn't feel her anymore.

"You're a liar, and I'm not raising a liar!" Her other hand went up and struck the other side of my head. Her blows were hard and direct. Jessie just sat at the other end of the table while this was happening. It's not like Jessie could really do anything, but Mother never struck Jessie, to my knowledge, his entire life. She loved him, and seemed to always want his approval.

"I'm not lying! I didn't take the cupcakes! He gave them to me. We were just talking after school and he gave them to me." My voice was shaky. I was talking through lips that had this wild stinging sensation going on. It was a funny feeling.

Her hand went up again as she put her face closer to mine. She struck the left side of my face again this time. My rigidly placed head didn't give to the sway. I just held tight.

"You're a liar, and you kids have ruined my life!" Her left hand went up then, slapping the other side of my head again.

Over and over she struck each side of my face while telling me I was nothing but trouble, nothing but a little ungrateful bitch that she bore the burden of raising. She hit me over and over, the slaps growing into blows from her fists. My head felt like a hollow melon, while Jessie sat at the other end of the table.

The sunbeams danced as my head swayed in non-reality. I no longer existed. The way the light looked was all there was.

"Now, you little lying bitch, you go to school and get out of my sight. When you come home, we're going to go have a talk with Carol and Aaron, and when they say you've lied, I'm going to beat you again."

She moved her chair back and continued with her coffee and cigarette like nothing had happened. I guess Jessie got up to go to school. I couldn't remember him anymore. I was absorbed by the heat in my swollen face.

I struggled to stand and balance myself. I thought my ears were bleeding. I had to get my school stuff. My brain muffled the reality. . .had to get to the bus stop. . . had to go into the world with a face that looked like it was bleeding.

Each step was fine, the stinging sensation was bizarre and interesting, it wasn't so bad really. It was the balance thing that I was adjusting to; it was the reality of the day I would have to live in that stunned me. It was hard to hide what Mother had done. She wanted the world to see what she had done. She wanted the world to know that I was worthless, that I was trash, and that I was nothing to be thought of.

Even in front of her, I acted like she didn't do what she was doing. After it was over, it was just over.

After school that day I went home where she waited for me. I was wishing she'd go back to work so that I could have some peace from her.

She marched over to Aunt Carol's house with me following behind her. She was still in one of her long, silky, blue green gowns. We went through the gate that she had put between the two properties.

My Aunt Carol lived in one of those small, readymade houses. Her lot was large and had a shed and garden in the back.

Aunt Carol opened the door. "Susan, you're making way too much of this! Please stop!"

"No, just get Aaron in here, and when he says this little bitch is lying, I'm going to beat her again. I don't care about her." I guess she had already told Aunt Carol that she had slapped me repeatedly that morning. Aunt Carol appeared mortified and in great despair for me. She had always cared for me, but would never stand up to my mother to save me.

"Susan, stop this, please!" Her voice was pleading, but weak and accepting.

My mother lit a cigarette, as I huddled at the other end of Aunt Carol's picnic table dining area. It was a very small area in her kitchen. I can't tell you what I felt. I think I was just enduring to see what would be, maybe trying not to think. Mother always had to take everything in her life to the greatest dramatic painful end.

Aaron came in, generally a nice but troubled boy. He took one look at us and his face fell.

Aunt Carol asked him, "Did you give Lizzy the cupcake, or did she take it?"

"I gave it to her," he said. Aunt Carol was mortified and apologizing to my mother as my mother waved her away and left the house. Apparently Aaron had gotten in trouble with Aunt Carol for sharing and had said that I took the cupcake, rather than saying he gave it to me. He was maybe eleven years old, and what kind of people count cupcakes, anyway?

To tell you the truth, I don't even remember the cupcake discussion with Aaron, and I didn't then. Maybe I talked him out of the cupcake because I wanted it, or maybe he just felt bad that I didn't have things like that to eat and offered it to me. Who in the world knew what would make my mother have another reason to do the things she did?

I went home and Mother was going through a stack of books on the table looking for something to read. She acted like I wasn't there and seemed perfectly fine. She went into her room and locked the door like she always did. I heard the steel fan running.

I sat on the sofa for a minute, contemplative maybe. Jessie passed through the room, but pretended he didn't notice me. After every time my mother beat me, no one would look at me. Maybe they despised themselves. I remember going to bed and just lying there, staring at the ceiling. The world was dark and cold, and stinging and trembly, and awful and lonely, and dark again... just dark.

5

KARO SYRUP

Jessie was sitting in the kitchen when I ran by in a hurry. I think I was happy; it was a beautiful sunny afternoon. I stopped in the kitchen pantry at the end of the hall to look for something to eat. I was nine.

As I rummaged through my mother's large pantry, the back of my hand knocked out a bottle of Karo syrup. The glass bottle exploded on the floor. My stomach did a flip into darkness, because I knew that in my mother's house, I wasn't allowed any accidents.

"You better clean that up, Lizzy, or Mama's going to whip you if she finds out you broke her syrup bottle."

"I will," I shuddered, as Jessie relayed the obvious. Syrup was slowly ebbing into wider dimensions around the broken glass.

I got the glass up and tried desperately to get the syrup off the floor. I had a wet rag, napkins, soap, but nothing would get up the sticky residue. I could see the sun coming through the front living room door, and it just made me sick.

"She's on her way home, she called a while ago, you better hurry up." He was matter of fact about my fate with Mother, which amazes me to look back on.

"Can you help me? I can't get the floor to not be sticky." By then I was panicked.

"Just wet another towel, that's all you can do."

I numbly went on. I think he was eating or something.

I was on my knees scrubbing like a crazed person when Jessie yelled out, "Mom's here, Lizzy! Hurry up! I just saw her car!"

My stomach flopped. I thought I was going to throw up. My knees were sticking to the floor.

"She's going to whip you, Lizzy! Hurry up!"

"Please help!" I begged, but it was too late.

"What the hell happened? Why are you on the floor?" Mother's voice came with a heavy boom. I felt like she was already standing over me, even when she was just at the front door. She was so broad that she almost completely blocked out the sun.

I looked up at her, "I accidentally knocked over the bottle of Karo syrup. I'm trying to get it off the floor."

"Well you better!" She stepped around me into the kitchen.

"Every time I walk in this house you've done something that cost me. All you ever do is cost me money."

Because of my stomach issues, my body started to tremble. It always did when Mother was around. My stomach was upset. I tried to control the upset. My body started to tremble.

She was in the kitchen one minute—Jessie said nothing—before she flew into her rage, and grabbed me up by my arm. She dragged me by the arm down the hall to her room so fast that I couldn't get my balance to walk with her, or run with her for that matter. She threw me over the bed and started beating me with her leather belt. She struck me from my neck all the way down my calves so many times that my body seemed like a blister of stinging sensations. My arms were streaked with red lines. So was my back when I raised my shirt in the mirror afterward.

She screamed while she beat me, "Don't move goddamn it, or I'll beat you harder. You're a nasty little tramp, and all you do is cost me money."

Every breath she took was labored. She was so heightened by the beating. When she was done, she grabbed me and flung me on the floor toward the door that led down the hall.

"Get your ass in there and get the goddamn syrup off the floor! If you don't, I'll beat you again!" She glared and her chest heaved from her exertion. I couldn't walk, so I crawled down the hall to where my rag lay on the kitchen floor. I don't know what Jessie was doing. I'd lost sight of him.

My body trembled as water streamed from my eyes, the release of pressure, nothing but. I had this soundless motion of cleaning the floor in a way that would stop her from having me live through again what I'd just lived through, but I knew I'd never clean the floor well enough to make her not beat me.

She never had mercy enough to kill me, which was probably what I wished for at that time of my life. She just wanted to beat me over and over again. She just wanted me to live in psychological horror.

When I felt the floor was clean, I got up to put the towels in the washer. I waited for the floor to dry so that I could walk over it and see if it was sticky. I'd cleaned the floor over and over for at least an hour, while she sat and smoked in the living room.

The floor was sticky when I tried to walk on it. An ache came over me. I knew I wouldn't escape her. That stomach thing wouldn't stop.

"I can't get the sticky up, no matter what I do," I told her from the kitchen as she came barreling in.

She walked on the floor barefoot, sticking to the floor with a tearing adhesive sound every time she raised her foot again. She was full of rage.

She dragged me back to her room and beat me again the same way she had before, before flinging me down the hall to try and clean it again. This went on and on, and I don't remember what finally made it all come to an end.

I just couldn't get the sticky up.

I never see a bottle of that syrup without remembering that day in my mother's house. Even in the grocery store, if I see a bottle, I feel a certain place on my shoulder twitch that got hit harder than the rest of my body. My left shoulder took some time to heal.

Once, when I was grown, in a moment of weakness, I reached out to touch a bottle. I just wanted to know that they made the bottle out of plastic now, or maybe I wanted to see if the glass was as cold as I remembered. But no matter, I studied the bottle that cost me a day in my life to Mother.

Before the bottle crashed to the floor, I was free and unbeaten inside. Or, at least I felt that way when I woke up that day. I'll never forget, though, how it all changed so suddenly, and how she was so broad that she totally blocked out the sun.

6

CHRISTMAS

Christmas was not my favorite time of year. Christmas was about my mother and how crazy she would go this time over the holidays. Mother bought gifts like crazy, for everyone, including myself. She took her credit cards to the limit and then complained all year about how she was paying off credit card debt from Christmas. She assured everyone around her that she would not run her credit cards up next year, especially since no one ever bought her anything good, or cared about what she may want.

"I spent two hundred and eighty dollars on Laura, and all she gave me was this cheap discount store sweater. I wouldn't wear that cheap piece of garbage for anything."

She would have the sweater on the table in its Christmas box for all to see, as she sat at her dining table with the usual coffee and cigarettes. She would mumble these laments to any in-and-out guest (and sometimes me) that would listen. People were always coming in and out of her front door. It was a revolving door of chaos.

Mostly, my older siblings ignored her. They knew that no matter what they bought, she would always be like this.

Every year she had to have a giant pity party until well into February. She liked the Christmas ammunition of bad gifts because it helped keep her unhappiness factor up and alive. It was physical proof of her bad and wasted life on ungrateful children, she claimed. She had to let the world constantly know that she was unloved, unappreciated, unhappy, and any other "un's" that could be possible.

No gift had ever passed the test for our mother, and no love ever did either. Mother could only love children when they were younger than three. I think it's because she knew they had no possible way of knowing her yet. She wouldn't trust them after age three. She would then start to pull away. We all saw this through several grandchildren.

I went to bed on Christmas Eve for many years with her screams and misery encircling me, engulfing me. She cooked a Christmas feast through most of the night that she just knew that no one would appreciate. She would drag me up, when she wanted company, whether she liked me or not. The breakdown actually began the evening before Christmas Eve on most years.

"I wonder what Quentin is going to get for me? I paid four hundred dollars for his rifle. I bet he just brings me something that he lets Laura get at the discount store. Laura's so cheap; I bet she buys something fine for her mother, though." She would ponder over her cigarettes and coffee. I wouldn't speak unless I was asked to. Usually she just wanted to complain without stopping for several days.

Jessie and Quentin were the two people that she really always made sure she spent her money on. She openly put them on a pedestal for the world to see. They never bought into her, though; they just tolerated her as we all did.

"I hate this time of year, all of you kids forget what I've done for you, all I ever did was try to make a family for you all, that's why I got married so many times. It was all for you all, it was never for me." I would be putting dishes away, or some other Cinderella task while she sat in her own unhappiness.

My mother's kitchen was a prison for me. After all the dinners of thirty in-and-out people, she would make me clean everything up; it went on for hours.

"No, no, Laura, Nicky. Don't clean that. Let Lizzy do that. You all just come on back and sit with me." Somehow Laura and the others were capable of that.

Christmas was a horrific time. My mother had an artificial tree that she had Quentin put up each year. When we were little, the tree had been a beautiful silver, but later it was a traditional green. Only one year did we have a real tree.

The year that my mother decided she wanted a real Christmas tree, I was eleven. She wanted to smell the scent of a real tree, she said. She talked about how it would deepen the meaning of Christmas to have a real tree.

It was just another one of her schemes, though, to find something that she didn't understand she'd lost. Mother wanted to fill the void inside of her, and I guess I can understand and appreciate that.

Mother bought her new real Christmas tree and had Quentin put it up for her. It was different; it had to be watered, and at first it did have a really unique smell. On Christmas Eve, though, Mother was doing her normal Christmas heartache routine.

"You are the worst kids! I shouldn't have ever married for you to have a family and a daddy! You're all ungrateful; you don't do anything for me!"

I just scrubbed dishes, and hid when I could. She had started hating the real tree she had bought, and the pine needles, days earlier. She had gotten into the habit of making me get down several times a day and pick up the terrible needles. I never did it fast enough or good enough.

"Get your ass out here; I'm sick of you hiding in your room. I'm on my feet day and night for you fucking ungrateful bastards. I've worked all my life and have poor health, for nothing!"

"You're a little bitch and I know you don't want to be out here with me. That's why I'll make you stand here till morning. I don't have to be nice to you! You're the worst problem in my life!" Her face was red and her massive fists were clinched, as she screamed in my direction. She made me kneel down and pick up needles by hand, then made me stand there silently until she made me kneel again. I never said a word. There was no need to. There was only the enduring, nothing else.

When I finally went to bed, at some unknown hour, she woke me by screaming my name. I searched to see where I was, as the sun coming through the window reminded me that I'd gone to bed, in my room, and it was Christmas morning.

"Did you know about this?" I looked at the pipe under the sink she pointed to. My stomach flipped again.

"Yes, ma'am," but I didn't quite get all of the ma'am out, before she charged me and caught me at my throat. She pulled me around, cutting off my air, and dropped me against the kitchen cabinet where the pipe was leaking. I kept swallowing, trying to make my throat feel the same again as it did before she squeezed it.

"Why didn't you tell me?" she yelled in my face. "All I do is slave for you kids and you can't even fucking tell me that the sink is leaking. It's rotting the boards because of you," she screamed.

"I could have fixed it long before it got this bad if you'd just told me! But you don't tell me anything, because you're a hateful little bitch." She grabbed me again and shoved me aside so hard that I crashed downward onto the kitchen floor.

"Why didn't you tell me?" she screamed down at me.

"I told Jessie! I just saw it the other day and I told Jessie about it!" Jessie was fourteen at the time.

"Why the hell didn't you tell me? Jessie doesn't make the money and slave to fix anything around here."

I was on my back trying to get off the floor, but I didn't know what to expect next, so I was going slowly.

"I thought it was okay to tell Jessie! The board was already like that when I saw it!" My throat was starting to feel normal, when my mother grabbed my wrist and yanked my body into the air. She slung me back toward the dining and living room area.

"Get your ass in the living room and get those pine needles up, or I'm going to beat you until you're bloody!"

I was on my knees as Quentin walked in. I listened to Mother fill him in on the horribleness of me. She never said anything about Jessie not telling her about the sink. She just made sure she told him about me. Quentin didn't say anything to me one way or the other.

Mother was screaming so loud as a few more people came through the front door to join us for Christmas that I was instinctively nervous. She was screaming about what I'd done to her life, and what a little bitch I was.

Eventually with four adults standing around, along with Jessie, she yanked me by my hair off my knees from the middle of the never ending pine needles. She took me by my hair and flung me into the dining room cabinets where she took both of her man hands and wrapped them against my throat.

My face was numbing from the pressure.

My mind had gone. She was off somewhere, screaming, "I hate you! You're nothing but trash!"

Her face was red. Her bulging eyes were right in my face, as her hands gripped my throat tighter.

"I'm gonna kill ya now! How bout that, you stupid tramp?

I'm gonna kill you now! What do you think about that?" She was taunting me.

My mind started to do this new floating thing. I couldn't get any air. My body was limp, suspended in the air. It was strange to have no command of my arms that swayed with her shakes.

Quentin and others eventually, after a very long time, started saying, "Stop it, Mama. You're going to have a heart attack!" Mother was always talking about her troubled heart. "Let her go, stop it!" I guess it had finally registered with them all that she might actually kill me.

"I want to kill her! I want to be rid of her!" Mother seemed to enjoy the act of being crazy in front of people.

Quentin finally just came over to get her off me as she dropped me from the air. She had to take everything to the end. My body fell like a rag doll, always, when falling from her grip. I was gasping for air in my lungs again as I lay there stunned, and quite out of my mind.

"Get your ass over there and get those needles up! I guess you'll go and tell your perfect daddy all about this, won't you? You tramp!" She marched off into the kitchen.

I saw her turn around and tell Quentin, "You better tell that tramp of a sister of yours that I have medical conditions that will get me off if I kill her! I can do anything I want! I can claim that I snapped and didn't know what I was doing." Everything had to be theatrical.

"Lizzy, she says she can claim temporary insanity," Quentin said, flatly. "Stay out of her way."

I crawled over to the pine needles. Tears streamed down my face from the release of pressure. My body shook with heaving motions, as everyone went into the kitchen to soothe our poor mistreated mother. I was glad to finally be alone.

I still can't look at, or smell, a live Christmas tree without thinking about that Christmas. After that, my father had me live with him for the rest of the sixth grade year. If he suddenly thought beyond himself, and had a heart, I will never know, but I really can't believe it. I was just the game piece in the life they wanted to live, and that was all.

I couldn't see anything beyond my mother and her rage.

AL

1

MEETING AL

Mother called Jessie, Brent, and me to her room one night when I was maybe seven. This was before her abusive years to me. She had gotten us out of bed; it was well after our bed time. She didn't know it, but we all had been awake. The boys were in my room. Jessie slept on the floor on a pallet, Brent was in the bed with me, and I didn't want him to be in bed with me, but I always felt that I had to do what he wanted.

Mother burst in on her children in the dark.

"Wake up, wake up, I have someone out here I want you to meet." She seemed very happy.

I heard his kindly voice in her room calling, "No, that's okay; you don't have to wake them up. I can meet them another day."

"No, No, they won't mind at all, come on guys, come into Mama's room."

We all just looked at her with a kid's mix of wonder and fear, and obeyed her. No one disobeyed her request ever. We knew they weren't requests. The false kindness in her voice sent chills through me every time.

The boys got up, stretched. No one said a word. My hair was cut short in what my mother called a pixie at the time. I slept in one of my normal little girl gowns. This gown was soft, white flannel, with a pale blue splotchy pattern running over it, and it reached mid thigh. My sleep attire changed dramatically after this year of my life. It's probably why I remember the gown so well.

I walked into my mother's room, not unsuspecting, and I pretended with innocent nature that I was a happy just awakened little girl. I saw him sitting on the edge of her bed. He was holding a huge tub of popcorn; they had just returned from a movie. I did not want the popcorn, though I knew I was going to have to pretend that I did.

Jessie and Brent dropped to the carpet. I was directed to come nearer to the man that my mother was putting on the show for. I knew I was supposed to say hello in a more personal way. I was also directed by her to sit on his lap. I supposed she was using me to win him over. I was always very small for my age, and seemed younger in nature because of my odd qualities.

"This is Al and I like him very much. I like him so much that I wanted to introduce him to you." Her voice was just so false that it made me feel icky. Not to mention the fact that this man was now offering popcorn to me and the boys that we had to act so thrilled to have. I just bobbled there on his knee; he had his arm around my waist, just holding me there.

We responded to Mother with the normal false nods of satisfaction, and told the man that we were happy to meet him. Her room was lit up, and I'd never been allowed in her room. I didn't like being there. The bedroom walls were dark brown panel board like the rest of the house. The carpet matched the rest of the house also, and along with her king size bed, adorned with a simple yellow bed spread, she had two dressers on different walls. There was an opening at one end of the room that led into a walk-in dressing room and bathroom. The worst thing about her room was the foil covered windows. When I saw the darkness from the hall, even in the middle of the day, it made me uncomfortable.

Al was blond, and a mid-sized man, I guess. I think maybe I could say that when we met him he seemed kind, but that was part of what he did to people; he made them think he was kind. I didn't honestly make an assessment of him. I was always so nervous with anyone new because I didn't know what people would do to me. It was a wait and see life.

We went back to bed. The boys went to their rooms. I was thankful that they did. I just lay there on my pillow, imagining another life, and people to play with that liked me and wanted to know me.

Three days later my mother called me into her forbidden room again. She had the radio on very loud. This joyful nature I'd see only when a new man would come into her life. I didn't trust it. I didn't trust her. I held one of my hanging down arms with my opposite hand. I was jumpy, nervous, watching her. What would she ask of me, without asking, today? I wore little girl jeans and a white T-shirt. Mother was heavily made-up, in jeans and a navy flowing blouse. She was passing back and forth from her sink to her make-up dresser and mirror that were filling the small dressing room.

She turned the music down when she noticed me.

"How did you like Al?" she asked me in a sing-song kind of voice that let me know that I was supposed to answer that I liked him, though I didn't know anything about him, and I was worried about what I would live through if she brought another man into the house.

I nodded my head with an apprehensive fake smile, "I liked him, he was nice."

"He liked you very much," she said then, like I should have been so thrilled about that.

I just smiled and kind of looked at my bare feet, waiting to be dismissed. I was jittery, wiggling my toes nervously. She loomed over me, and her perfume, that was the finest, just made me sick.

She started going back and forth again from her sink to her dresser.

"He's so wonderful and kind, Lizzy. He wants to marry me." I knew those words were coming. This was husband number seven. She would have nine before she stopped getting divorced and married.

"What do you think about that, Lizzy?" She turned and paused to look at my face.

I did my pretend smile and didn't know what to say. It didn't matter; she already knew what she would say.

"Lizzy, do you think I should marry him?" My eyes looked up and caught hers involuntarily. I didn't know what to say.

"Would you like me to marry him, Lizzy?" She moved in on me, looming once again. "It would mean a daddy for you. He loves little girls."

Still looking at her, I nodded softly, weakly, "Yes, I think you should marry him." My pretend smile was starting to make me feel crazy.

"Well, you can call him "Daddy," you know. I think it's best if you do." I was scared then. She had forced me to call her last husband "Daddy." Jessie had refused and could stand up to her. All I could think of was my own father and how I loved him. I didn't want to be disloyal to him.

"Do you think you can call him "Daddy" for me?" She had gone back to staring at herself in the mirror.

"Okay, Mama, okay." I thought I was allowed to go when at that moment she turned the music up to go back into her own world.

I had this feeling in my stomach of unease that I lived with for so many years. I walked down the hall slowly tracing my fingers over the panel board. I stood at the end of the hall staring out at everything in the world she created. I just didn't see an end to her world, and I didn't know how to live or die.

2

THE RED WATER PUMP

In my dreams I sometimes walk through a winter wood. It's the deepest forest, and in my child's heart, at seven, I'm only skeptical of my surroundings. I walk slowly. The sun sometimes stings my eyes from certain angles. It's only from the sun's angle, with partial cover, that I see the red water pump.

The water pump is an object that I wasn't familiar with except on TV, and even in my child's mind I wonder why it's there, in the woods, in the middle of nowhere, and in my dreams, but when I did remember the red water pump in my life, outside of my dreams, my heart hurt, but not for myself, but for life, and what life had done.

I walk through my little girl dreams, in a t-shirt, in the dead of winter, my arms stretched out above my head, not feeling the cold, but it is hard to feel anything. Feeling just isn't a part of thought. I don't feel made for feeling. I feel that I am a spectator.

Mother married Al, and I didn't see anyone any more. In my mind the whole world disappeared, except for Al. Al just kind of took me out of anyone's radar that would have thought to call my name, or think of me, even in malice. He was everywhere I was, always redirecting my life into his life. Jessie disappeared for good during this time. He never knew me again. That was it.

Life turned into Al. He was everywhere. I was invisible, a non-being. He flashed a smile, and as charismatic as he was, the world was cheered. No one ever questioned what he might have been doing, always alone with me, a seven year old girl, always taking me out of radar. I lived in the South, where people feigned ignorance. There was an understanding to not understand, to not take responsibility, for the things you acted like you didn't see that were going on around you. It was a hard-to-stomach life.

"Lizzy, do you want to drive?" The car vibrated on the dirt road so badly that my body vibrated in time with it.

I smiled a brilliant fake smile, while eating a chocolate bar. "I can't drive. I can't even reach the pedals."

In a whispery voice he said then, "Don't worry about it. I can do the pedals for you."

Al was taking Jessie, Brent, and myself fishing for the day to get to know us better, and Al and I were going to get more bait, or this is what he told the boys. He left them fishing off a bridge in the woods, the same woods that still exist for me in my dreams.

I kept smiling, "No, I don't want to drive." I knew even at this age that I didn't want to drive with him. I knew something was going to happen with him, but I didn't know what it was or when it was going to happen. I can't explain the knowing, except to say that his behaviors were similar to other behaviors that I can't recall. It's like I knew generally what men were going to do with me, and I hoped inside, each time, that it wouldn't happen this time.

"Oh, come on," he cheered. Come sit in my lap and I'll let you drive." Something in his face, in his voice, told me it wasn't a choice, and I did as I was told. He was blonde, with a perfect boyish grin. I can't look at men today with boyish faces without turning away instinctively. I'll have to work on that.

I put my candy bar down. My stomach had turned, and I climbed into his lap to drive. I acted like all was happy, just like I was supposed to. I tried to drive while he talked on and on. He coached the driving, and talked about how he was so happy to have a real family, and to have a little girl of his own.

I could feel him underneath my bottom. He was hard already, and I knew somehow that I was supposed to notice. I acted like I didn't, but that was part of the excitement for him, too. I felt this sinking feeling at seven, and I wondered how long he would stay. Mother didn't stay with a man very long. Maybe this time she wouldn't either.

"Can I tell you a secret?" he cheered again.

"Sure," I said, because I knew I was supposed to say that.

"Oh, no, I can't tell you my secret, you might tell." He laughed a little.

"No, I won't," and he had no idea that I knew the game and would not tell. The game made me feel tired, and I didn't remember why I knew the game. I felt so sick to my stomach.

"Yes, you will tell."

I flatly said, "No, I won't," as he guided the car off the road, deep into the woods, where there was not a soul for miles around.

"Okay, I'm going to tell you my secret." His smile turned into a conspiratorial one as I slid off his lap.

I was small and he was big. I could see his face from turning glances as he talked. I stared straight ahead as much as possible, and felt the flush of sadness and fear take over me. I didn't know how I was going to get out of this and avoid him until my mother was done with him.

I nodded.

"You can't tell anyone," he said. "Not your mother, the boys, anyone! Do you understand? Do you promise?"

"Yes," I said, flatly. "Yes, I understand…I promise."

"Are you sure?" he asked again. I was trying to act like I didn't notice that he was touching himself and then taking himself out of his khakis. He had backed himself more against the door, facing me. I sat with my body forward, trying to cope, wondering how long it would last. I was trying to act like I didn't notice the agitation in his voice.

"I'm sure." I looked at my dangling legs and dirty jeans. I leaned forward with my elbows on my knees.

"This is my secret. I want you to be my special friend. I want you to give me your hand." I felt trembly and sick suddenly as I sat up, and stretched out my hand. He took my hand and put it on him.

"This time, I just want you to feel it," he directed. "I just want you to feel me."

My hand was limp where he put it. "Go ahead, feel me." From the sound in his voice I knew it wasn't a request. I knew I had to do what he said, but I didn't know what to do. He took my hand and rubbed it on himself. He seemed to like that. He tried to squeeze my hand around him and move my hand up and down.

I don't know how long he made me do this before he let us go get the bait and go back to the boys.

The thing I remember most about that day with Al was something that happened inside of me while I sat there. As he sat back to do the stuff he was doing, I just had this sense of becoming smaller and smaller. I felt like I was the size of a pinhead carrying around a giant body.

No more could I imagine staring up at my tiny fingers, translucent from the rays of the sun. I still felt in awe of life, but I no longer felt my personal fingers were worth examining. Something about that day, in the woods, with Al, and seeing a red water pump, through the glass, behind his back, just set me apart from myself in a way that nothing else before it had.

The size of a pinhead. Isn't that so confusing?

3

NIGHT TIME

I remember seeing my mother only twice during the Al times. Once was on Christmas Day, a short time after she married Al. I say a short time, because I still remember trying to figure out how to live on that Christmas Day. She, or they, had gotten me a Pink Panther bike for Christmas. It was a Santa thing, and I woke up to the new bike, and watched my mother watch me, as I pretended to be so happy about it. I knew it was my job to pretend that I liked the bike.

Al was like a shadow over me. He built a perimeter around me where I knew that it wasn't just Mother I was pretending for anymore, it was for him, and what he had created. He constantly reminded me that I wasn't supposed to let anyone know what we were doing. He said he would be very disappointed if I let him down.

He held the bike in the yard in front of Mother's cinderblock porch, and pushed me off while I played the part of the excited kid, happy about Christmas. I rode the bike around while hearing her tell my sister-in-law, Laura, how much I loved Al and how much Al loved me and how he wanted to get the bike for me. I was tired and I felt anxiety every moment.

Mother was bartending through the night in those days at the local lodge, and Al kept the kids away to give her some days off for rest.

I spent nights in the room that I hated and feared, my mother's room, with Al, on my mother's bed.

He would force me to come into the room with him in the night. Most nights he would wait until everyone went to sleep to come and force me to go with him. I learned to fear the sound of my bedroom door as he opened it.

"Lizzy, are you awake?" I held my breath as he touched my shoulder. I pretended I was asleep.

112

"Lizzy, wake up." He knew I was faking being asleep, I think.

I turned over as guided by his hand on my shoulder. He slid me over and lay down under my covers with me. I knew he didn't have on any pants. I held myself together the best that I could.

"Let's go in the other room, Lizzy."

"I'm really tired. I have to go to school tomorrow."

"It won't take long. Come on now." I knew it wasn't a request.

I followed him to my mother's room. He made me take my panties off. He would place me very specifically on the edge of her queen sized bed.

"Now, scoot to the edge." (I wasn't there with him. I went somewhere else in my head.) I scooted to the edge of the bed. He took off his clothes. I don't remember what his form looked like.

The room was lamp lit. I saw the white sheets that I had to lie on and the yellow bedspread pulled down. Mother's dressers seemed huge to me. Her steel fan was my enemy, even though it wasn't on. The fan was her, and she was evil.

I clutched my tiny hands to my chest, holding my night gown up and in place.

"I know you love this," he would say.

I gave no expression. I was trying to stay away from myself. I was okay at the moment with being the size of the head of a pin.

His body hung over mine. He had his right hand by my shoulder stabilizing himself on the bed. His left knee was beside my thigh, bracing him.

"Look at it," he would say, referring to his hardness in his hand. I did as I was told without seeing him really. I learned to act like I was there without being there.

"You want it, don't you?" I didn't move. I learned that he didn't always notice when I didn't respond. I learned to know when I had to.

"Come on, you know you want it. You're just pretending that you don't, but it's okay, I know you want it." I had no understanding of what he was doing. He seemed to be a slave to himself, to his sickness.

"I'm going to put it up inside of you as far as I can but it's not going to hurt you. I'll stop when it won't go in any further. You're going to guide me."

I felt sweat across my forehead, and my head pressing back hard to be further from him on the bed. I was trembling all over from some unnamable fear. He mistook my shaking for excitement somehow, and this I could not understand.

He lowered himself and pressed himself up against me.

"Does that hurt?"

"No," I said it fast, disengaging.

He pressed harder, and then released the pressure. He did this over and over again. What I realized after the first few times that he did this is that he just stayed at the open place between my legs. He couldn't actually go in any further. Each time I was violently afraid of what was going to happen, but then learned the way of things so that I could mentally escape.

"I know you love this," he would say. His breathing was funny; his voice was agitated.

When it was over, he would act like he had done this great thing somehow. He would tell me to go pee it out. I didn't understand what I was supposed to pee out. I was aware that when he was finished he had wet me all over between my legs.

Sometimes he would come to my room and I would make it clear that I was just too tired and that I would do it another night, but then he would get angry and tell me that he did everything for me and that I did nothing for him.

It was very hard for me. I then felt guilty and went and did what he wanted. Somehow, his feelings were more valuable than mine.

I would look at my Raggedy Ann lamp, on my bedside.

I was afraid of the dark. Sometimes he would turn my light out, leaving me alone in the darkness, shut my door hard and loud, and I just didn't know what to do.

4

AWAY FROM HOME

The second time I saw Mother, during the Al times, she was sitting like a catatonic on the living room sofa. It was this ugly flower-patterned, brown, black and white sofa that blended in with the same colors in the living room carpet.

I would walk by her sitting there staring straight ahead, in her silky blue/green nightgown, and I would know that she was faking a breakdown, again, for whatever attention she had decided she needed. I was too much in tune to her now at age eight for me not to feel what she was doing. I don't know really what I thought, except for the feeling I had that she disgusted me.

Al had come to my room that morning. He had been abusing me so long by then that I lived in terrible despair. I was scared each second just waiting for the next bad thing he would make me do. I was afraid to be in my room at night because he would come get me. I would go days without sleeping.

By then, my head was so confused that I wasn't just afraid of Al. I had an ongoing fear that other people would come to my room during the night while I slept. I stopped sleeping and woke panicked if I accidentally fell asleep.

I stood at my long short white dresser that went along the opposite wall of the bed. I looked at Raggedy Ann, and missed a book I'd had about her and Andy when I was little. The room was so small that other than the dresser and bed there was only walking space to my closet at the end of the room.

When Al came in the room, I felt my face tighten. It wasn't the normal kind of day, since I had expected him to be gone that day, and I was disappointed. He pulled my arm to have me come face him as he sat on the edge of my bed.

"We need to talk, Lizzy." His voice sounded like he thought he was this great, thoughtful person in my life. It was very confusing, and I just stared at him, unable to pretend any kind of kindness towards him anymore.

"What's wrong, Lizzy?" He was acting sympathetic like he wasn't hurting me all of the time. I just stared at him still.

He lost patience with me but still kept some composure. I guessed he knew that Mother could possibly hear the conversation from the living room. At that point I had no idea that she was even out there. She had given me to Al.

"Lizzy, I'm taking you to stay with me at this house I've been remodeling in town. The boys are going, too. Your mother is having a hard time and she needs time to rest."

I started to tremble all over at the prospect of having to go live with Al somewhere.

"I don't want to go," I looked up forcibly.

"What?" he looked like that was an insane response.

"I don't want to go," I said again. I felt my arm rhythmically shaking under the pressure of the grip he had on my forearm.

"What do you mean, you don't want to go, Lizzy? After all I do for you?"

"I don't want to go!" I said again, quite clear and loud. I felt hot tears streaming down my face.

"Get your stuff together, Lizzy! You're going. I'll be back in a minute to get you." He shut the door. I sat and cried, not knowing what to do anymore. I just didn't know how to make it all end. I felt so sick. The sickness just did not go away. I couldn't bear the idea of there being no chance of escaping him.

My tears didn't last very long; they were a release of tension when they happened. I didn't understand them, and I always felt separated from emotional feeling.

When he came to get me out of my room, I went as I was expected. There were no choices in such a dead place. I just had to do what I was told. At the end of the hall and turning to my right to go to the front door, that's when I saw her sitting there to the left, out of the corner of my eye. As I said, she looked like a catatonic.

I didn't fully understand what I was seeing in her at that time. I know I had a complete feeling of disbelief over what was actually happening to me. I think, also, the feelings I had were maybe subtle realizations of her choosing her life over mine. She had no inclination to ever know me or protect me from anything.

Maybe I also felt disbelief that Al could fall for her act, but then as I got older I realized that he was fine with what she was doing. He got to make a wife of an eight year old girl who was scared to death, literally trembling with fear all of the time. How wonderful that must have been for him.

The home Al was renovating was near the fairgrounds in our small Southern town. I can't drive near that area today, even though I don't remember where the house is, without having the feeling that the whole world is closing in around me. I've tried to fight the feeling, but I can't face that part of my life yet.

He sat me down in the master bedroom of the partially finished house and told me that this was our bedroom and that I was his wife now. I just stared deadly when forced to acknowledge. I didn't have any feeling left but sickness. When forced to speak, I just didn't know how to fake anything anymore. But…I found it didn't matter.

Al had it in his mind what he thought I should feel and that was all that he cared about. He decided that I felt this way or that, and sometimes told me that's what I felt; he said that I just didn't know that I felt that way.

There was not much in the house. The boys had the only other room that had a mattress in it. There was a table in the center of the kitchen where we all ate, but the living room had no furniture, and the carpets were ripped up.

One night Al was trying to get me to have some form of sex with him and I just wouldn't, so he told me with what I would have described as a child's tantrum voice that I could just go sleep with the boys and that he was sick of doing everything for me and my doing nothing for him. For the life of me I couldn't figure out what it was that he felt that he did for me. I know I felt guilty when he said that, but I didn't know what he did for me.

I wandered through the house, avoiding falling on boards. The boys' room was at the other end of the house. I had to walk through a sawdust-strewn living room and through the very small kitchen to get to where they were. I stopped when I reached the boys' open door. I stood in the archway watching the light from the window above their heads light up the room.

I turned away, but I didn't cry. It was just survival.

If I lay with the boys, Brent would make me do sexual things with him.

I felt sick. I didn't know how to remove myself mentally from Brent's behaviors anymore, and so the lesser of two evils was to go back and do what Al wanted. At least with Al I could remove my mind very well. With Brent it would have been like starting a new abuse all over again, like learning to cope all over again. It was all unbearable.

On top of everything else, Al was so delighted on my return in the dark, that he kept telling me, all during his rubbing himself all over my eight year old body, that he just knew how much I wanted him all along. He said I was just playing hard to get, and that he'd forgive me.

He never let me go anywhere with Jessie anymore. One day while we were in the house towards the beginning, Al was busy with work at another house and had to leave Jessie and me home alone. I had the best day just walking all over the fairgrounds with Jessie, but Al never let me go again.

"Can I go with Jessie? He's going walking." I was kind of pleading.

"No, sweetie, let the boys go. That's no place for you." His voice was cheery, like the world was such a beautiful and perfect place. I felt ill and wasted in my own invisible form.

"You get to help me around here today." He smiled and ushered the boys out.

He lay on top of me, in the afternoon light, me on the edge of the black comforter, rigid and gone. He didn't even notice. He just kept telling me how much I liked it. I heard him saying it as I lay in a distant world.

He was the enemy, pushing his body up against mine. I didn't know what to do and there was no end in sight, especially if Mother was going to take time out to be crazy on the other side of town.

Going to school when Al was around was hard, too. He would often keep me out of school, while he would take the day off from work, so that he could have sex with me in various ways throughout the day. I remember him sitting in front of my school, me in third grade.

"I don't want you to go to school today. Let's take the day off and be together." I just didn't understand his acting like I was a grown up, but I had to play along for survival.

We sat in front of my elementary school office, in his big brown truck that he had gotten from my brother, trading him for the dreaded car that all of this started in.

"Well," my voice was shaky and trying to sound pleasant, "I can't miss school today. I have this big test to take, maybe another day." I remember trying to seem so natural, while feeling the fact that I was so close to getting away from him.

"No, I want us to spend the day together." He would act like a person in a tantrum again, but with a broad grin, on a boyish forty something face. He was confusing to me. His face, his expressions, did too many contradictory things. They didn't match anything that I could understand or reason out.

I was still trying to sound nice. "I can't do it today. I have a test today."

And sometimes…his response would be…, "Well, okay, if you have a test, you have a test," and then he would let me go.

But other times he was mean. He would rant, "Well, you never do anything for me. I do everything for you and you do nothing for me," and then I would give in and have to go with him, missing school, out of some sense of being guilty that started in his mind and poisoned my own.

This was a battle, most of my days, with Al. I needed school. It was my only escape from Al, but I couldn't even rely on that escape.

The hardest part I think now is looking back and knowing that on the days that he let me escape him, he totally meant to let me escape, and the days that he wanted to do what he wanted, he was never going to take "no" for an answer. It's the hardest part, I think, because of realizing how truly trapped I was.

He must have known that there were no real tests in the third grade, but he liked watching me try to squirm my way out of being with him, when he already knew whether he would let me escape or not. It's hard to know that he was getting off on what he was doing to me, hard to know that he was enjoying pretending to weigh my choices, when I really had none at all.

5

ANOTHER WORLD

In Al's monopolizing of my life, I'd lost all sense of being alive outside of him. I don't know how it happened. Life became this dark tunnel I wandered through with my hands dragging along the walls. There had been a time, right before that first time in the car, when I still knew that there was something other than Al in the world, but any knowing of that had vanished. It was such an astonishing thing to me—that I could evaporate, and become so incredibly small.

Even though I never remember seeing my mother in all of this, I do remember that she had a wonderful friend. One night, this friend, Mrs. Weston, wanted me to spend the night with her, apparently after Mother and Al had dinner with her.

I had gone away from my life so much that I only have some fragmented memories of her place.

The adults must have had dinner. I remember Mrs. Weston, her husband, and Al being there that particular evening. I do not remember my mother, though she was there. Al decided he needed to run an errand; it was nine o'clock at night. I don't know what the errand was, but I had to go too. Maybe it was to take the boys to a late night movie, something he had planned to do in order to get to be alone with me, while Mother was occupied with her friends.

Before picking up the boys, Al stopped at a store, bought beer, and forced me to buy candy. I didn't want candy, and he never drank beer. I have a glimpse of Jessie in the living room, mad about the candy, and Al telling him he would get him some, not to worry.

The next glimpse of a memory I have is being in the truck, in the woods, with Al. He wanted me to drink the beer. He wanted me to pretend that I was a grown up. I couldn't drink much. I was dying inside, it was dark, and the woods and Al were a coffin that I'd come to know.

He did what he always did. He made me take my clothes off, but this time holding a beer bottle. He took his pants down and began what he began with me. I was naked and cold. The night was black and wet. He'd parked us so deep in the woods that leaves and branches beat at the truck windows.

When we got back to Mrs. Weston's, I stumbled into the door; I don't think I pulled off normalcy that night. Al kept telling them that I just didn't feel well.

Mrs. Weston had me sleep in her room with her that night because I was ill. I went to bed before her. My stomach was going crazy. I kept needing to go to the bathroom because my stomach was torn apart. I think I dreamed at one point that I was in the bathroom and that it was okay to use it. I don't know why my body didn't go to the real bathroom. I wasn't so asleep that I couldn't.

Mrs. Weston found me. I was between sleep and awake. I didn't feel shame even that she found me that way. My worries were well beyond her reality. She helped me shower; she cleaned everything up, with perfect grace. She never said anything to me about it, and she never told my mother.

I would always store and keep files on people that were like Mrs. Weston. Whatever the case, kind and responsible people like Mrs. Weston lived in a world that I was not privileged to know and live within. I think if I had been present in my life then I might have been sad about that fact, but instead I just waded through the cold, dark tunnel, stunned by a remarkable existence, and didn't know how to know that life should have actually been something different.

I didn't know how to wish that I was in Mrs. Weston's world. That baffles me today, the fact that I was so dead, too dead, even, to wish and dream. I went inward. I just shrank more deeply into the nothingness of me.

6

MY FATHER'S VISIT

A l became the world around me. I was caught in an "Alice in Wonderland" kind of mind.

Al came into my life when I was seven, almost eight. I'd had several years to adjust to my father being gone, but I never did because of the life I lived with Mother. I missed my father so much that I remember a few times in my life thinking I'd seen him, and then going up to someone and realizing it wasn't my father.

Once, I thought I heard Jessie say, "Dad's outside," but when I ran out to the truck, it wasn't Dad at all. It was one of Aunt Carol's old husbands who used to make me sit on his lap while he touched me.

I had gone to the door after Jessie said Dad was outside. I looked at the truck and the man standing outside of it. It wasn't my father, but I just knew, in my mind, that it was. I saw that it was my father as clear as day. I believed it with everything that was inside of me.

I ran hard out to the driveway, and hugged the man tightly without looking up at first, but his voice and the feel of him wasn't right. I was slowly in those seconds registering that the man had a different voice, the man was shorter, and then when I looked up at his face, I let go of him in a quiet shock. It was the man that had lived next door. He thought I was so happy to see him. I was confused about my ability to believe so hard about something, and make it so in my mind. I was scared of myself.

The next time I thought I saw my father was when I'd gone to work with my mother. She was bartending. I stepped into the barroom, and this older gentleman in a hat was saying hello to me as I entered the room. I only saw my father's face. I ran up and hugged him, only to have the identical thing happen that had happened with Aunt Carol's old husband. I was scared of myself because of my ability to believe in the altered reality.

I was ill through the years, in and out of hospitals. One time, during the Al time, I became so sick that the doctor told my mother that if I didn't stay in a vaporized room that I would have to go into the hospital again, and be in a special tent.

Because Mother was not in my mind, I don't remember her telling me about staying in my room, but I know that she must have, because I can hear her voice in my head: "Lizzy, don't open this door, don't go into the boy's room, and no one can come in here! If you do, you will have to go into the hospital! I mean it! Don't let me catch you outside of this room!"

Next thing I remember is my standing in the back room doorway.

"Lizzy, Mama's gonna be mad, you better go back to your room!" Jessie's voice sounded muffled and far away.

"Can I play with you two?" My voice sounded like it was coming from someone else's mouth. Brent and Jessie were playing a board game on the floor in their room.

"No, Lizzy, go back to your room!" Jessie was stern. I don't remember Brent ever being verbal.

"I don't like it in there; I don't know what to do in there." I stood barefooted in a night gown, rubbing my sweaty forehead.

"Do what you want Lizzy, but Mama's gonna be mad!" He went back to his board game. I walked across the floor and sat in front of the game for a few minutes before returning to the heated room.

I must have fallen asleep; I know it was the middle of the night. Four people were at my bedside in the dark. There was a light in the hallway that put just enough light in the room for me to see that there were people in my room. I know the people were my mother, Al, Claire, (Dad's next wife in line after Joy,) and my dad. They were on their knees beside me.

I did make out the faces of Claire and Mother with a blur. I saw my father and had a longing inside of myself for him that was too big for me somehow. I thought, "It doesn't matter that he's here, he's not really here, no one's ever going to be with me again."

Al's face was cooing in my face, ebbing backwards and forwards as I tried to focus on my father. Al's face seemed three times bigger than the other faces. Al's face seemed to be to the left of the three people, and then to the right of them, but then he stood behind and above them all. His grin had a message for me, his cooing had a message for me.

I got the message: "Focus on Al, never focus on anyone else again. Don't slip up, remember our secret, this is evil fun, don't slip up in the dark!" His mind spoke to my mind. I could hear him.

I felt myself pretending to be happy to see all of them, with Al looming in his crazed distraction.

They left. I didn't have my father, and that was it.

Al came in and leered at me in his insanity, "Good night, Lizzy. Now wasn't that nice for them to stop by and see you?"

I just stared at him. He always acted like everything was perfectly normal. The air was getting hot again from the vaporizer with the door shut. Al left the room after patting me as I held tightly to my light green bed cover. I hated his hands.

I couldn't tell anymore what was real and what wasn't real. I had trouble knowing if I was awake, or if I was asleep in a dream that I couldn't wake from. I didn't understand this very physical life form that I had become, so concrete, but not. I longed for the time when I floated in translucence, even though I may not have been fully conscious of my longings.

My mind was a place that I wanted to leave behind, but somehow I was still made to live in it.

7

SUNNIE

I had a dog I loved, when I was young. She was a beagle mix, and her name was Sunnie. She was light brown, with a splash of white across her nose.

I'd sit on my mother's front porch steps and Sunnie would come around the house to greet me. It delighted me to see her rounding the end of the trailer, coming through the side gate, and wagging her tail, all the way to where I was.

Sunnie never licked me when she came up to me. I always thought that was a superior trait that she wasn't a licker, but she did always want to sit right up against me. She liked when I put my face against hers. I loved to kiss her as she averted her face. I thought it was funny.

I picked the bright orange berries from the bushes that went around the chainlink fence in my mother's big front yard, (berries you didn't eat,) with Sunnie sitting beside me. I sat and played with azaleas that grew wild along that same fence, with Sunnie sitting along with me. When I would stretch my arms out and spin until I fell with dizziness, Sunnie would just watch me like I was an idiot, and come sit on me when I fell. Sunnie was very dear to me.

I worried about Sunnie a lot, though, because my mother wouldn't buy her food. My Aunt May used to say that Sunnie found her own food as she wandered the neighborhood in those days. I was never sure if Aunt May just said that to make me feel better, so I worried just the same.

I'd taken to giving Sunnie things I could scavenge from the kitchen, which wasn't much. I remember once even putting bread in a bowl of milk to see if she would eat that. I remember a neighbor on the other side of the fence making fun of me once, and asking me what I was feeding her. I lay awake at night worrying if she was hungry or not.

I carried on in odd ways with Sunnie. Sometimes I would hug her really tight, but then I would push her away, and then, in the same motion, I would grab her and tell her I was so sorry that I did that to her and hug her really tight again. I never knew why I did this. Now I understand that I did it because I was trying to make sense of life, trying to make it understandable somehow.

When I was apologizing to Sunnie, that I'd mistreated her by pushing her away, I did so profusely and desperately. It was funny: Sunnie endured the hug, and kept herself unmovable except for a slide as I pushed her away, and then accepted my hug again. In all, I don't think she really noticed or cared what I was doing. She just always moved close to me again, except for once when I did it about four times and then I saw that she didn't rush back over. That made me desperate, so I just forced her to sit close to me again.

I had pretend conversations with Sunnie. I don't remember what we talked about; I just remember my being silly. Maybe I'd pretend to be different people that I'd seen around me, just to hear my own voice out loud. I did odd things like that.

When Al had established himself in my life, and I had to endure the circumstances of that, he was always trying to buy me things like candy, but candy always made me sick at that time. I was too confused to be able to enjoy candy of any kind, but Al never stopped pressuring me to take things he bought, or forcing me to choose something in a store, so that he could look like he was treating me well.

One time I had a plan. I was sitting outside with Sunnie. I realized while worrying about her hunger that I could finally do something about it. I realized that I finally had the power to feed her.

I jumped up, went in the living room where Al was, and waited for him to ask me what I wanted. I was a head down, distracted kind of kid.

"Lizzy, do you need something?" He was getting up to go into the kitchen. It was a Saturday and he wasn't working.

"Sunnie needs dog food," I blurted out.

"Okay," he said as he dug into his pockets for a few dollars for me to go to the corner store.

I quickly said thank you, and ran out the door with Sunnie

following behind me down the porch steps. I remember feeding her the dog food on the porch when I got home. I was so happy for her, but I also remember feeling so much shame for reasons that I couldn't really understand. I knew that Al had given me something, so I had to give him something, and that's all I really knew at the time.

Al was gone when Sunnie died. I remember my mother putting on an embarrassing show of how she just couldn't tell her children such a thing as the dog had died, or talk to us about the delightful, and joyful, doggy heaven. Everything was a terrible, glorious, put-on show with my mother. She had to experience life in the most false and dramatic ways possible. She was the ruin of us all, in those days.

Mother called us to her room, and in came Laura, Quentin's wife.

"Lizzy, Jessie, your mom wanted me to come talk to you about something." Laura's voice was always soft and quiet. Jessie and I just stared at her. We knew Mother was acting false for some reason and we couldn't figure out what horror she would bring into our lives this time.

"There was an accident last night, and I'm afraid that Sunnie was hit by a car." Laura was deeply grieved to be telling us this. Jessie and I said nothing. Mother just sat back on the bed, enjoying reveling in a true life moment.

"Sunnie's in dog heaven now, she's with other dogs, maybe her mother and father. I think she's happy to be there." Laura was so young; her skin was porcelain like an angel's.

I don't remember what I thought about her words. I don't know what I believed about dog heaven. I do remember thinking that she was making a point that it was a different heaven from humans and that didn't settle well. It just made me not want to think or believe in heaven at all if it was arranged to separate me from my dog. Sunnie's spirit was no less valuable than my own. People were always so confusing for me.

"Do you have any questions? Would you like to talk about it? She's buried in the back yard now. Would you like to see where she is buried?" Jessie and I were silent, while our mother was drooling over her angelic prize daughter-in-law.

I declined visiting Sunnie's grave right away. I wanted to go alone.

I don't remember a time in my life after her death when I didn't think of Sunnie when I stepped out back where she lay in that mound of dirt that eventually leveled down. Sometimes I would go stand around it. Sometimes I would talk around it. Sometimes I would pick my berries and azalea blossoms and go sit where she was now.

The one thing that I knew for sure and that I was very ashamed of is that I was glad she wouldn't be hungry anymore. It just hurt so much to live with Sunnie's hunger every day.

8

LITTLE HOUSE ON THE PRAIRIE

I lay on Aunt May's double bed under a dark green bedspread. She was living with us for a while, and I was hoping to hide from Al in her room sometimes while she was there.

Little House was about to start. That night's Little House was about a young girl who lived alone with her father. The girl's mother had run off and the father was obsessed with the young girl's not being a bad woman like he felt her mother was. I remember to this day how that father looked at the early developing young girl. He was telling her to wrap herself tighter at her chest. I think in the show it became apparent to him that boys liked his daughter.

The young girl in this episode of Little House was attacked and raped by a masked person in the woods on her way home from school, more than once, I think. Her father's house looked to be deep in the woods. The strange relationship she had with her father, along with the violence the girl had experienced, made me start trembling.

I lay under the green bedspread, thinking there was no mercy for me, even on Little House. Everything was black.

I watched as the young girl became pregnant. I watched how she fainted at school leaving class one afternoon. I watched how she got sick with the pregnancy and couldn't control it. I watched how she died in the show from a fall. I trembled under the bedspread. I started to sweat. Aunt May asked if I needed another blanket. I shook my head no, as she got more concerned.

Al called from the hall, "Lizzy, can you come here a minute?" I wouldn't go.

Al called again, seeming irritated. "Lizzy, come here, please." I didn't go.

Then Aunt May said it, "Lizzy, he's the only person that's good to you here. Why are you so rude to him?" Her frustration was clear, and I no longer looked at her in the same way.

Every day after that, I woke up wondering when they were going to find out that I was pregnant. I waited to faint at school. I was careful not to fall down for fear of death. Every time I had a stomach ache, I knew it was the baby making me sick.

I carried that imaginary baby so deeply that I didn't recall my Aunt May beyond that day until I was told she died one summer while I was away. I just tuned out her existence.

I didn't find out I wasn't pregnant, so I carried that imaginary baby inside of me for months and months. I wasn't in touch with reality and I didn't know about human biology.

I could have carried that baby a thousand years. I felt ashamed of me, and thought at any moment I could turn up pregnant.

I was standing by the monkey bars at school when a little girl my age was talking about her older sister's possible pregnancy.

"My sister might be pregnant, and my mamma doesn't know!" Kimie had a lively animated face. She had squinty blue eyes and rough, blonde hair.

My ears perked up, "What do you mean?" I asked.

"She was with a boy and they did it, so she might be pregnant!" She looked at me like I was an idiot. Kimie had four older sisters.

"How exactly does a person know they might have a baby?" I stumbled with the question.

"What?" Kimie was exasperated. "He put his you know what inside of her you know what, and that makes a baby!"

"So, a baby only happens when that happens?" I felt my face burn red hot. Al couldn't put his whole thing inside of me. He had tried but I was too little.

"No, not just that. A girl has to have a period first! Then, if she's with a boy she could have a baby."

"What is a period?"

"Good Grief, Lizzy! A period is something a girl gets when she's a teenager, it's blood that comes once a month. It only lasts a few days!"

"Oh." My body relaxed all over with possibility. "You mean you can't get pregnant until that comes? Are you sure?"

"Of course I'm sure! My mama's going to be so mad!" Kimie was always in her own stratosphere. I loved that about her. She was one of the only girls that had befriended me at that time in my life. I had elaborate fantasies, fearing that she wouldn't like me anymore when she found out I was pregnant, and then I would be alone again.

I felt such relief at not being pregnant.

9

MOTHER FINDS OUT

My mother drove a burgundy Oldsmobile for a time. It's the car I remember her driving the day she asked me about Al. She had a new car every few years. She held on to nothing and reconstructed herself continually over the years through cars, husbands, and major trailer renovations.

I sat in her car, in white soft shorts and a blue t-shirt. I didn't feel like I wanted to know anything about myself anymore. I didn't care anything about anything anymore. I just lay against the passenger seat door with my forehead on the cool glass while my mother drove us home from the grocery store.

I was startled, and sat up straight in the burgundy seat when she started to talk. My mother didn't talk to me; she ignored me, unless she was giving me orders or verbally abusing me. While driving, she was usually deep in her own head, listening to the country and western station. I didn't like the music; it was too representative of what she was in those days, full of misery and troubles and loneliness.

The music was off on our drive and I didn't know why it was off, but I didn't really care. I was just trying not to come out of my skin, which is the way I felt all of the time. I felt something welling up unpredictably inside of me that I just don't have words for. I was trapped in an existence that was going to hurt me no matter what I did. I'd gone from seven, to eight, to eighty in what seemed like an overnight transition. The only thing going in my favor was that Al was away for a week or so doing some job out of town.

"Lizzy, did Al ever do anything to you?" I bolted up straight, leaving my quiet comfortable spot against the door.

"No!" I shrieked it out like she was crazy for asking.

"Are you sure he never touched you or anything?" She slowed her driving. Fear and panic made me so sick that I wanted to throw up.

"No, no, he didn't, why are you asking me this?"

"I found out some things about him that I didn't know before, Lizzy. He's gone; he's not coming back from the job he took." She stared at me intensely. I just wanted to get her focus off of me.

My voice was a whisper, "He didn't do anything to me." I leaned back against the door again, my head pressed against the glass, my stomach giving way to sickness and upset. I felt like the sickness would never go away.

Then a horrible feeling swept over me. She was going to find out what was going on with Al. I felt that it was my fault what Al was doing, and I just knew that she was going to find out what I did. I began to sob quietly then. I just knew there was no way out for me. I looked down at my ugly dirty feet in flip flops and hated my ugliness.

"What is it Lizzy?" she immediately pulled the car over.

"Nothing!" I cried.

"Lizzy," she panicked. "Was there any blood?"

I panicked then. I didn't understand her and the question of blood.

"No, there wasn't any blood." My voice wasn't tearful, because the shock of what she asked went through me so hard.

"Are you sure there wasn't any blood?"

I was frustrated and scared then. She was the enemy and I knew it.

"No, there wasn't any blood. You won't tell anybody will you?" I panicked and started asking this over and over again.

"Of course I won't, of course I won't," she promised me that she wouldn't tell anyone.

"Please don't tell Jessie, or Daddy, or anyone," I then begged.

"I won't tell anyone, I promise, I won't tell anyone. Everything's going to be fine, Lizzy. It's okay now. He's gone. I won't let him hurt you again."

We seemed to be talking as equals in that moment. It was bizarre. I was demanding secrecy and she was complying in that moment, it seemed.

There was no more discussion as we drove home. We were back

to our normal selves, me with my head against the door, and her being in her own head. I was confused when she turned the car into her lodge. It was one of the family lodges, always full of people from the time it opened in the early afternoon.

"What are we doing?" I asked. "I thought we had to take the groceries home."

"We're just going to stop in here for a minute. Lock your door when you get out."

"You're not going to tell anyone are you? You promised you wouldn't tell anyone!" I was out of my mind with shame.

"No, I'm not going to tell anyone, Lizzy."

The lodge bar room was huge, dark, and smoky. The bar itself was shaped like a giant horse-shoe, taking up a third of the space in the middle of the room. The seats all around the bar were taken. There must have been forty people seated around it. The juke box wasn't on when my mother sat me down at a little round table that faced the bar.

Mother had on a silky brown blouse and light brown pants as I watched her walk to the first people at the beginning of the bar seats. I watched my mother, for an unnamed amount of time, go to each and every person there.

I saw her crying, while people were looking back at me, as they were consoling her.

My mother, who said that she would never tell anyone what happened to me, was telling people what had happened to me. She was rolling in the sympathy of others while I sat there completely and utterly ashamed of who I was. I couldn't hide from the stares and looks of those people.

I knew my mother was a liar, and the enemy, but I think maybe I did think she would have had sense enough not to have made me watch what a liar she was.

We drove home in silence. She was in her own excitement of attention now. I was home ten minutes before she called me to her hated dressing room.

"Lizzy, come in here," she called like it was Christmas Eve.

"Yes?" I walked in and answered. I hated her guts and if I had been older I probably would have wished she were dead.

This was a turning point in my life. I had so much hatred of her and hatred of myself that I wasn't even afraid of her anymore. Something inside of me where she was concerned had shifted.

"Get some better clothes on. We're going to have to go tell your dad what happened." She was loving doing this, and I couldn't quite understand why at the time.

"What!?" I wailed out, panicked. "I'm not going to tell him! I'm never going to tell him!"

She didn't even see me. She was making herself up in the dressing room mirror. "Lizzy, your father has to know, and we're going to go tell him."

"You said you wouldn't tell anyone and I watched you tell everyone at the lodge. I'm not telling him." I started to turn away.

"Yes, you will tell him," she finally looked at me pointedly. "He won't not love you anymore. He has to know. Go get dressed." She wasn't even her crazy, don't talk back to me or I'll kill you, self. She was getting off on the information she was carrying to my father.

I would have been afraid of my mother, but I had nothing left to lose. After this stage of my life at eight, almost nine, I would avoid my mother's turbulence because of what it cost me, but she would never be able to make me afraid of her again. I don't know why this was. I can't figure it out, but I just hated her, and had nothing to lose, and that was it for me and her.

We sat at a restaurant in broad daylight. When my father came in, he just looked like there couldn't have been a worse time in the world for him to have to meet with us. He was in uniform and had been working. He also couldn't stand my mother.

We were all seated when Mother put on her most syrupy voice.

"Lizzy has something to tell you and she's afraid you won't love her anymore if she tells you."

She tried to touch me, but I scooted away from her fake poisonous touch. It registered with her that I wasn't letting her get his attention using me, and I was glad.

"Now, Lizzy, don't pull away, everything's going to be okay."

I hated her!

"I don't have anything to tell him," I looked straight at her when I said it. Then I looked over at him and watched how he looked completely uncomfortable and out of place with us. He didn't want to be there, and he seemed more uncomfortable for himself than worried for me.

"He won't stop loving you, Lizzy." She sounded syrupy and sick.

"I don't think he will. I have nothing to tell." I looked down and away from both of them then. I was defeated by the incredibleness of them both.

"Al has been doing things with Lizzy. Inappropriate things." I felt pinhead small and ashamed. I was ashamed of me and ashamed of her. I looked up once and saw the weakness of character in his face. He just wanted to get out of there as quickly as he could.

"Tell her you won't stop loving her," she said in her syrupy voice. I was slumped down in the seat real low.

I watched him stumble over the words, and then he let us know that he would talk with us later, he had to get back to work then. We never talked about it again, and I didn't want to.

My mother told the world what happened to me. No one in my family ever looked at me the same way again. I was tainted, not quite right, in their eyes, I felt. The worst part was when she talked about what happened to me to other people in front me, like I wasn't there. She didn't care how things felt for me. She just reveled in the gloriousness of getting attention for herself.

She ruined me. I already knew early on that I was damaged, different, and felt that something was seriously wrong with me. I can't tell you what it did to me when she laid me out in full public view like that. I needed to be the only one who knew that I was what I was: something bad. I was ashamed and humiliated on whole new levels.

Al was a pedophile. He had been in prison before for abusing children. Mother married Al and knew nothing about him. Someone came in the lodge bar one night who knew Al's past and told my mother and her friends. That's why she started questioning me.

My mother's self-absorption had created my life with Al, and her self-centeredness ended it.

10

STUNG BY BEES

After Al, Jessie barely let me go anywhere with him anymore. He didn't want me around. His tones with me changed. He acted like he didn't see me walking in a room, and if he did, he had a look of disgust and anger. I don't remember a calm word that passed between us after that. This time began his eighteen years of silence towards me.

Mother told me that Jessie said that what happened wasn't Al's fault, but that it was mine. Jessie thought Al was very kind.

"Jessie says there's no way he would ever believe you about what happened with Al." I felt her own questioning in my mother's voice as she sat smoking in the living room.

"Sit down here a minute." She pointed one heavy finger at the sofa across from her.

"Yes, ma'am." I sat on her huge, multi-colored, expensive couch. When I sat on the edge of the middle cushion, I had to stabilize myself, the sofa was so big.

"Well, that's what Jessie said. He said Al didn't do anything to you, and that you wanted what happened." She was very matter of fact, without an ounce of restraint. She was enjoying her cigarette. She seemed to enjoy watching the smoke leaving her mouth. I would turn and stare at the dark burgundy sheers she had placed over the two windows in the room.

I sat silently, not knowing what to say. I felt very dirty. Mother, who promised not to tell anyone, had told everyone. She had taken us, the children, out to dinner with my Uncle Jacob and my cousin Sara, and we had all sat at a round table, and she and Uncle Jacob discussed it all openly, in front of us, the four silent children at the table.

Mother had made a point to tell all of the family in my presence, and talk about Al and me together extensively. When in front of people outside of the family, she had discussed it like she was the victim of this awful thing that had happened to her precious little girl.

I didn't say anything, still, to my mother, who was chain-smoking in her big chair.

"All I'm saying," she repeated again, "is that Jessie doesn't believe that it was Al's fault!" She was a little sneery then.

I honest to God did not know what to say to my mother.

"Yes, ma'am" was what eked from my throat, finally. I guess that was good enough for her. She then turned back to a book she had been reading. I guessed that I was free to go. I waded down the hall, to my boxy little room, with my finger dragging slowly down the ridged, brown, paneling board.

What was there to say? Jessie had seen what Brent was doing with me in the boy's backroom, so now he believed that this was apparently my thing. There was also some other reason in my brain as to why I knew Jessie thought it was my fault, but I can never bring it to the surface. It's just one of those things, lost in time.

Jessie thought I was bad. I thought I was bad. Mother certainly thought I was bad. I felt shrunken in my mother's dark house. I felt that even the trees outside the windows were whispering my name. Where I didn't have personal inner feelings, I had developed the knowing of shame, outright and upfront. Other people seemed to take up space. I just floated and couldn't grasp whether or not my life was truly real.

One afternoon, in early fall, Jessie allowed me to follow him fishing. I did not beg to go, so I don't really know why I ended up on this particular trip. It was a beautiful day; we walked under the huge forest trees without a word. The sun came down through the leaves, and I felt happy, like I was remembering something good that used to be. I don't remember much about Jessie really. I think, in all that happened, he was becoming invisible in my world, like so many others had.

On the way back from fishing, I was dragging my feet through the leaves, under the trees. I was just enjoying the sounds that the brown crisp leaves made with their movement. Jessie said once, "Lizzy, you shouldn't drag your feet, take higher steps."

All of a sudden, out of nowhere, I was swarmed by stinging bees.

"Run, Lizzy, Run!" Jessie shouted at the top of his lungs. He was well away from me and moving fast.

I finally outran the bees or they lost interest and I caught up to Jessie, but I'd been stung multiple times on my bare legs and arms.

"Let me see, Lizzy." I stood there silently, frantically rubbing down my arms. I didn't show upset feelings. I didn't know the appropriate way to act. The stings were jolting me, though, and it felt like the bees were still biting me.

"Mom's not home. We'll have to take you to Aunt Carol's. Let's go." He rushed through the woods, grabbing all of his fishing gear as he went, with me following.

When we reached our street, I remember the sky having a quality to it that wasn't registering with me. I spent a lot of time alone. I spent a lot of time with my mind in the sky. I lived in my head, and I often spent time imagining I was a tiny being that lived on the leaves of giant beautiful tree branches.

The sky was dense blue, like it wanted to think about rain, but no rain was about. My physical being was quite at a loss. The stinging was gone in my brain. That was easy. Jessie was panicky, but I was no longer there.

I saw my mother's home, in panoramic mystery. I kept hearing this loud clamp sound, like the sudden clamp of a huge metal door. There were no clouds, and Mr. Revel's house seemed closer than it really was. My hands seemed not to belong to me, dangling at my dirty sides.

Jessie walked with me up Aunt Carol's porch steps, leaving his fishing gear on the other side of the house. Her tiny square porch was four or five steps up. "We can tell her about the bee stings, Lizzy!"

Jessie was standing on the porch knocking at Aunt Carol's door. I waited. I was registering the black paint beneath my feet, and the black steps I'd just come up.

I looked up at Jessie again. He kept knocking, but then, suddenly, I was standing alone!

I wasn't coherent enough to understand that Jessie was there, but then he was gone. In later life I would remember that Jessie zipped by me in a whirring motion, but in that moment, I was very stuck on wondering what had happened to Jessie.

I started clasping my arms, then, my body going backwards towards the steps.

Al stood in the doorway.

"Well hey, Lizzy, how are you, little darling?" The familiar grin came at me. He seemed so tall that he must have been ducking under the shrinking porch roof. He loomed over me as his arms grew longer.

"Lizzy, have you been doing okay? I've missed you so much, honey!" His voice was dripping sweet, he seemed to be purring, and I was inch by inch going backward in slow motion.

I don't know what I looked like standing there, the bees forgotten. I know I didn't have a voice.

"Well, I'm going to go back inside now, sweetie. I'm so glad that you came over to see me!"

"Okay," I must have nodded, as his large luminous figure had to squat and squeeze to get back inside of Aunt Carol's minuscule front door. I turned on the edge of the steps, went down and around the house. I sat alone for a second, just breathing. I had no thoughts, except, "Wasn't Jessie just here, what happened to Jessie, wasn't Jessie just here?"

I didn't go home. I had no home. I walked to the sand dunes to hide. I don't remember anything that happened after that.

Al ended up marrying Aunt Carol's lonely sister, Edna. Edna was very kind. I don't know why grownups, even nice ones, do what they do. Maybe she didn't know about Al, either.

Mother also told me that Aunt Carol didn't believe me, and maybe she didn't, I don't know. Aunt Carol was always so good to me, so this was very confusing. Maybe she didn't tell her sister about Al because she didn't believe what happened to me.

The sad fact was, Al, who had gone to prison before, had to go to prison again. Not that I'm sad that he went to jail again, but I'm sad about why he went to jail again. I want him to be in jail forever.

He went to jail because he was caught trying to molest Edna's nine year old granddaughter.

11

ASKING ABOUT AL

I'm putting my experiences on paper, like I remember time, and God knows, I don't remember time. Once, early in my work with my counselor, she asked me to go to my mother and get some clarity about what had happened and when. My counselor had no idea about my mother.

In my mid-twenties, in the periods of time when I still came in and out of my family's lives, it was not strange for me to just pop up out of nowhere after long bouts of lapsed time. My mother would simply ask me where I'd been and complain that, after all she had done to raise me, I was horribly ungrateful for not coming to see her more often. She had completely blocked out everything she had ever done to me or any of the others.

I found her on the great cement porch that stretched almost the length of her doublewide. It was two cinder blocks high with an awning covering it fully. It wasn't screened in and the awning was held up by thin metal columns all around it. Mother sat in her old bleached-out rocker, in one of her silky blue/green gowns, just staring out into the starlit night sky.

She didn't seem to notice my arrival. All sound from the outside world was muffled to her because she had planted great fir trees that grew tall above the trailer, creating a border around herself and her yard. She said when she planted the trees that she just didn't want people to be able to see her anymore, and that she wanted to be alone. I understood her, and not being a cruel person, said nothing. After all, if I'd been her, wouldn't I have wanted to plant trees all around myself?

It was all odd, her choice to plant the trees, and perfectly fitting. You drove into a bright, normal neighborhood, but one of the houses was pitched behind a dark forest, as if her home existed in the middle of a forgotten bad dream.

Mother didn't move when she saw me. Her expression didn't change. She just kept up her slow methodical rocking. She had a way of holding both her hands below her elbows, kind of holding herself. I thought the look made her seem vulnerable, but I knew who she was, so maybe it was just the entire picture of an old woman rocking on a hidden porch and clutching herself that made her appear vulnerable.

I walked up two cinderblock steps; the porch was painted gray in these later years. I took a seat in the spare rocker next to my mother.

"It's been a long time?" She didn't look at me when she spoke.

I looked over the midnight yard, midnight because of the trees. The sky seemed supremely luminous because of the darkness of the yard.

"Yes, ma'am, it's been a long time."

"It's not right the way you don't visit me, and after all I've done for you and the rest." She seemed beaten down, lower, more introspective than usual, to me. I was confused by it, though she had always spent all of her life in her own head.

"Yes ma'am, you're right." I never contradicted her and told her that she didn't do the things that she claimed she did. To do so now would just seem like shameful behavior in front of her broken demeanor.

"Are you back again, or is this just for tonight?" she asked.

"I don't know, Mama. I think it's just for tonight." I was always confused on some level when she would try to lure me in through my lack of loyalty to her. Sometimes I wanted to act like she didn't do so much damage to me and just bury my face in her silky blue/green nightgown.

I never did this. After childhood, though, I wasn't afraid to be near her physically anymore. She seemed powerless now.

"What are you doing now? How's work?" she asked me, and kept rocking. I could see the paint on the porch floor being rubbed by the weighted down rocker. I kept watching for the paint to chip, but it didn't.

"Everything's fine, Mama." Neither of us dared make eye contact in those days. I laid my keys down gently on the concrete floor and put my hands together in my lap.

"Mama, I need you to tell me when you were married to Al."

Her body became vividly rigid. "Why do you want to bring that up? It was a long time ago. Let it go!" Her hands started a familiar wringing in her lap.

"Mama, I can't let it go. I'm seeing a counselor who's trying to help me move past the bad things. I have to get my times and memories in order so I can do that."

"I don't want to talk about this."

"Just tell me when you were married to him." I felt uncontrollably hostile. I watched her then as she stared away from me. I wanted to stop the wringing of her hands.

"I wasn't married to him long." She sounded like a coward.

"When was it, and how long?"

"I don't remember. It wasn't that long!"

If I'd been older, I would have understood that she kept saying it wasn't for very long because that's how she comforted herself with what she had allowed to happen to me.

"Was I seven, was I eight? Was it a year, was it two? Tell me anything that will help me know my life!" I felt panicky. "I don't blame you for my life; just tell me what I need to know."

"It wasn't a year. It wasn't that long." She looked down on her wringing hands, noticed them, and went quiet.

"Okay. Thank you. Now, can you tell me the dates? I'm not trying to hurt you." I softened to her age, to her only vulnerability.

She stopped rocking, and looked into my eyes.

"You could have told me," she blurted out, like she was going to stand her ground with me. "I was the kind of mother you could tell!"

"WHAT!" The back of my hand flew up to cover my mouth. I jumped up out of my chair and backed up a couple of feet to the metal awning support. I held it so tight I looked up once and saw my knuckles were white. "What do you mean?"

"You could have told me! I was a mother that you could tell!" She was openly blaming me for what had happened.

I calmed down. "Mama, what happened to me wasn't your fault, but you have at least got to know that you were not a mother I could tell." She stared off into space and I tried a different approach. "Mama, what happened wasn't your fault; kids don't tell their parents when this kind of thing happens. They just don't. Did you tell Grandma what happened to you?"

"No, that was different. She was not a mother you could tell. She made me go off with my uncle on Sunday afternoons, and she knew what he was doing to me. She would tell me, 'Be nice to your uncle now, he buys you new shoes.'"

"I'm sorry that happened to you. I'm sorry that Grandma was so bad, but kids don't tell, Mama. That's nobody's fault." I squatted in front of her holding onto the rail.

If I had been older, I would have realized the pain that I had caused my mother by this visit, and I would have understood that she did feel that she had done a better job with me than her mother had done with her. It probably horrified her in the end to realize that she had allowed any of what happened to me with Al to happen, when she thought, maybe, she was doing things right. She most certainly wished that she had been told, I think.

I guess she spent the last years of her life in a great deal of pain, directing her hurt toward me, the daughter who didn't stop her from becoming her mother. Anything but that.

ON THE RIVER

1

THE GODS OF WATER

Growing up, we wailed to the gods of water…, to the gods of absent light…, and to the gods of lawless, loveless children, because, God knows, all we had was each other, and whatever River God was watching over us at the time, some mystical being that whispered: "Even though you are forgotten, you are, however, truly meant to be alive. I give you voice, I give you the air, and I'll give you a reason to love it here…, you won't even know why, but you will love it here, in this life."

I jumped into the warm bay in the snuggest life jacket my father could find. I was five. I think if our father could've floated a helium balloon above my head he would have done it. It didn't matter to me, though. I just jumped with the rest of the kids. We swam at the old marina from dock to dock, by moonlight alone. We weaved around boats, we weren't afraid to die, we weren't afraid of anything; it felt good to not be afraid.

"Jessie, Jessie, where are you?" I called, breathless, hoping I'd beat him to the dock we were racing to.

"I'm already up here," Jessie would cry out with delight. I never really cared that much about winning.

There was no longer a cabin on the river when our parents divorced. Our mother had given it to a friend, without our father's consent, and it was gone, just like that. That's the family story. She turned it over to a friend. Maybe it was hers to begin with, I don't know.

So after that, Dad brought us to the small river community marina where the cabin had been, with a small camper and tents. We camped on the beach side of the marina, overlooking to the north the bay and its channels, and to the south, the never ending ocean. I was fonder of the never-ending ocean. I was that kind of kid. I loved that there was no answer to it, and that it was as old as forever. The ocean was my friend; I couldn't separate myself from it.

Water, boats, and our father—he would always live on the water, one way or another; he was made that way. At every stop from our town to the small town marina where he kept his boat, people loved him; they loved to see him coming. At every stop he also bought me a grape soda, as if there were any way in the world I could've drunk a soda to match his every beer. He made about three stops in the forty-five minutes it took to get to the river. Most times we would stop at each place and I would watch him talk to the people inside. Jessie would watch him, too, if he happened to be with us.

I was so happy on my father's boat. I used to sit under the top bar on the front of his boat and scream, "Faster, Daddy, faster! Make it splash, Daddy," at the top of my lungs. He always complied. He made the boat bounce on waves and splash my feet. Being on that boat was the best time of my life. I was the kid with the bright orange, extra tight life jacket. No one knew why I wasn't allowed to be without one but me and him. I was the kid that didn't try to come back up.

But, I did not like Joy, Dad's new wife. She was scary to me. One day Joy said that I had done something wrong. I forget what, but she said that I had to get a spanking. Joy had my father do it.

Joy had my father give me the first and only spanking that he'd ever given me in my life. This is the only memory I have of the woman, and her platinum blonde beehive hairdo, with her overly made-up face.

I don't think they lasted very long, our father and Joy. Her house was cold, too white and too sterile, in my child's mind. But, I was just a child. I really knew nothing about Joy.

I was so glad to get to come to the ocean and be with my father, but the strangeness of Joy was a lot to cope with.

"Lizzy, come here, please." My father's voice was at the other end of the polished living room, in the too white house they had in the suburbs. We had just driven back from the marina, and I had forgotten that Joy had told me I would get a spanking.

"Yes, sir," I complied in my small voice.

He took my hand and led me to the bathroom. He knelt down in front of me.

"Lizzy, you have to get a spanking now, because Joy said you weren't listening to her. She said you repeatedly ignored what she asked you to do." He stared into my eyes, painfully. His voice was soft and nervous, whispery even. His eyes looked worried.

"Yes, sir," I sputtered.

I looked down at the beige bathroom carpet and sucked my fingers. "Lizzy, are you going to listen to Joy when she tells you not to do something?" I continued sucking my fingers like he wasn't there. His hands were around my waist.

"Lizzy, you have to listen to Joy." His voice seemed shaky.

"Well, Lizzy, I won't spank you very hard. Let's just make her believe you got a good spanking, okay?" I felt my eyes widen as I sucked my fingers harder. I wobbled on my legs.

"Look at me, Lizzy." I looked up, without expression, without feeling, without any acknowledgement in the world. I felt like I was floating above myself. His head jolted back slightly from my motionless expression.

"I'm going to give you two taps on your bottom, okay?" I nodded my head, and he popped my bottom twice. It was my heart that hurt, but my childish mind didn't understand why. He was so upset that he told me to wash my face and he left the room. I felt bad for him.

I was a floating object. I didn't know how to feel bad for myself.

2

CLAIRE

I literally staggered out the door to my father's truck when he came to get me that Christmas Day after the incident with my mother's sink. The street wasn't alive with children in the early afternoon as it had been in recent years on Christmas. I had a bag that wasn't too heavy to carry. I didn't own much, but my body was heavy to carry. My muscles ached; my mother had already doomed herself to her bedroom for the day. She had ruined Christmas for everyone with her insane tantrum over the leak in the kitchen sink.

The sun was so high and bright in the sky that it hurt to perceive it. On Mitchell Drive, we threw away the sun. We longed for darkness. We lost our lives, but we didn't mean to. We lived with, and within, our broken minds.

Every day that we do not live is a waste. Every day was a waste, and I did hurt for that reason. That Christmas was silent; Jessie was a half centimeter space in my thoughts, minuscule, and something else that my mind had banished. He didn't want me, and I never imposed. I couldn't ever see forcing my presence on people.

I clutched my bag, the screendoor creaked. It should have been night and the events of the day would have made more sense. I still had Mother's fingerprints around my throat when my father, the false light, arrived to pick me up for a few days of Christmas break.

When my father got out of the truck in the driveway, he stood by the door, waiting for me to come to him. He would step no closer. He took my bag from me, saying, "Lizzy, why is your shirt buttoned up so high? Can you breathe? Undo it." Even though it was winter, I guess I did look odd in my blue cotton shirt buttoned up so tight around my throat. Maybe it had something to do with the fact that my shirt was way too small for me anyway.

149

"I know you'll tell him!" she had screamed an hour earlier, like it was her last breath to be taken. She always acted like that.

"No I won't," I had mumbled into nothingness, but she had kept screaming at me anyway. She always knew, though, that the price was too high for me to ever dream of telling anyone the things that went on in her house.

I didn't know, sitting in my father's truck that day, that later someone would report to him that he should not send me back to my mother. Someone who saw her attack me had thought that she would surely kill me.

When I got into my father's truck, I could rely on a few good things. One was that my father's world was the opposite world of my mother's. He did nothing to harm me, and would do nothing to harm me. A sense of relief went through my entire being as I sat in the front seat of his truck, put my head back, and listened to Johnny Mathis.

The next thing I could rely on was a completely energizing peaceful existence on the water for several days before I had to go back to my mother's again. I loved the water the way that my father did. The power of it always drew me to it like nothing else in the world. I had immense respect for it, and I knew I belonged in this part of nature.

The most wonderful aspect of my father that I could rely on was his absolutely calm character. We would make our first beer stop just a ways out of town, and my father would take me in to talk to all of his friends for a bit. He gave me grape soda. When I grew out of it in later years, he still insisted that his little girl have a grape soda. He was funny that way. He didn't accept change well, except for the latest sporty vehicle on the market, which he kept to perfection until the day he traded it in for the next model.

Whenever he would pick me up after he got off work, he would take off his police uniform shirt, fold it perfectly, and tuck it away behind the seat, before he took a beer from the ice chest that was always in the back of his truck, for the long drive home. He'd have some button down shirt to go over his white t-shirt, a beer, perfectly cuffed pants and shiny black shoes.

That day, as always, we made our several stops on the way to what was now a house he had built in a neighborhood on the river, near where our cabin used to be. After years of camping, he'd finally decided to just buy a house in the small fishing community. He knew everyone, and everyone knew him.

At this time in his life, our father was married to Claire. She was an investment counselor, and she was one of those women who was so pretty and sweet that it made you pause. She was glamorous, regal even. Claire was perfectly dressed; she had perfect hair, perfect makeup, and beautiful dark tanned skin. Her dark hair and eyes were stunning, and she had this way of moving that was full of graceful sway. When she walked into a room, everyone turned to see this woman, just to watch the presence that she had. She was soft spoken, and never had to raise her voice. Everyone wanted to please her.

Claire and our father had built the house in the river community immediately after they were together. From what I knew of Claire, I had no complaints about her. Jessie hated her after a few visits that he'd gone on without me, when, for some reason, I'd had to stay at home.

Jessie said that Claire lied about him. She told our father that Jessie would do the most ridiculous things, like rip her plants out of the pots around the house, or that he had cursed at her. No one would believe Jessie would ever do anything like this, after the way that we were raised. Children in our time didn't do anything to adults without the price being too high to pay. But Jessie stopped going to see our father.

When I arrived at my father's that day, I was met with the warmest welcome from Claire. I was naturally leery of people, so I just nodded at her kindnesses, and did as I was told. I wasn't privy at home to any real information about her. What I knew about Claire, I'd overheard.

A few days later, after my father had been told about what my mother had done to me on Christmas, he talked to me about living there with him and Claire. Claire was happy and encouraging. I was such a reserved child that I didn't ask questions about anything that was going on. He told me that he'd heard what had happened with Mother, but I didn't add any information.

At one point Claire tried to ask me what happened with my mother. She appeared gossipy, excited over the information. I didn't understand her eagerness for information. Everyone knew you didn't talk about Mother; it was an unspoken rule. Claire was new; she didn't get it. Her behavior was odd in those moments, not regal. She quickly appeared more ordinary.

3

THE RIVER COMMUNITY

The river community was simple and quiet. My world revolved around one long street that started with a gas station and a major bridge at one end. There was the old marina in the middle of the street a few miles down from the gas station where my siblings and I camped with my father on the beach side when we were little, and a couple of miles after that was my father's house, in a small neighborhood. Part of the neighborhood was directly on the bay.

Rod's Marina had always been a happy place for me. The old steel blue and white striped building was a place to play all of the days of my life that I'd been allowed to be there. Even being there for a day showed me there was something to live for. The place was heaven. Everyone knew us in this river community; everyone said hello; everyone was so happy to see us. All of the little old ladies had to pinch my cheeks and look directly into my face. "Yes, what a beautiful child you are," they would exclaim. "Honey, those brown eyes are gorgeous!" I would laugh out loud.

I didn't know who I was when I was on the river, because I was so alive there. I was okay with people when I was there. It was my father's energy that dictated what it would be like in this part of my life. I noticed that he treated me like anyone would treat a child, and that the people around him followed suit. I also noticed that he was delighted and proud of how well behaved I was. He always had been. He probably didn't really think about why I was painfully good. I believe good behavior was the expectation in general.

The marina had a bridge in the road beside it, where the river flowed underneath to the other side of the street. I spent many hours with nets, trying to catch fish that were far too deep in the water to be caught. I also loved to run up and down the boat docks that ran parallel to the roadway bridge. I spent hours watching the intense lives of crabs, who insisted the marina sea walls must be their home.

On late evenings, I'd see my father as the sun was setting coming up the road to get me and bring me home. He put my bike in the back of the truck, told me it was time for dinner, and we went. I always stayed within the parameters set for me. He always knew where to find me.

I was enrolled in school that sixth grade year with my father. The river community school was very strict. I remember getting a demerit for not pushing my chair in one morning. If you got five demerits in a week you got spanked before you went home on Friday. No one had to ever tell me anything twice. I'd spent my life avoiding negative consequences.

I made all A's, except for a B, in math, at the river community school. The school was known for being the best and most disciplined around at that time, even to neighboring communities. I don't know that I was proud of the report cards I brought home, because I didn't know how to be proud of myself. I just knew that if I messed up at all I was going to get demerits and be spanked. I was afraid to miss any assignments; missing an assignment meant a demerit. I watched other kids line up for their Friday spanking, and I could not let myself be one of them.

It was different to me for me to know someone was going to hit me. My mother had always just snatched me up, out of the blue. Somehow, that seemed better to me than the planning to be whipped.

The house on stilts, which is how I described it, was brown and blended into the trees and landscape. Lots of houses near the water are built up high. My father's had a party room underneath the house; the upstairs was small with two bedrooms. It was a delightful, cottagey little place, with a wraparound deck in the tree tops. I enjoyed it very much.

Our neighbors on Till Road were mostly elderly. I had quite a few close friends that year who were elderly. I made daily rounds to say hi. I would walk to the Rays who lived next door to Dad's house, when they were home; they only stayed there at certain times of the year. Mr. Ray had only one arm. He made jokes about it all the time. Their house was made of cinderblocks that were painted yellow; it always felt damp and cold in their house. The smell was funny when they would come in and air the house out after being gone for a while.

Next I would see the Scotts, if they were in town. They lived a ways behind my father's house, on land that wasn't quite cleared yet. They had a camper they brought when they came in. They were planning their retirement home on the property. I'd sit and talk with them a while, hear about their grandchildren, things like that.

The Harpers had one of my favorite places to bike to around the neighborhood, because they had a deck that hung over the water with trees growing up into it. It was fun to go hang out on their deck and eat cookies. Mrs. Mildred liked giving me Oreos, while her husband told me stories about where they came from up north.

On my way down the street, past our neighborhood, towards the marina, was my father's best friend, Mr. Neil. Mr. Neil had a huge commercial garage on the street, for any mechanical needs, boats, cars. He and his wife, Mrs. Shirley, had eleven mean yipping little Chihuahuas at their house. I always stopped to talk to them when they were outside.

"How are you, little Lizzy? What are you doing with your day?" Mr. Neil would ask, giving me his complete rapt attention.

"Oh, I'm fine. I'm going to see Mr. Rob today." Mr. Rob had a house on the canal that was further up.

"Well, I think he has a doctor's appointment in town today, but you go try him anyway." His speech was high and clear. His smile, though it was slow, was so kind.

Mr. Rob was my favorite! I walked up the steps to his house on stilts over the canal, where I was welcomed into a world of stories. I couldn't get enough. He was handsome, strong, intelligent. He mesmerized me. He had been an airline pilot most of his life. He talked about being in the war, while feeding me chocolate bars. He talked about his children and grandchildren. He was delightful. His home was very masculine and classy. He cooked, and I watched him cook, sitting at his small kitchen bar. He had a shop down the road, on the bay side, where he had different hobbies going on with his grandson. I can't explain exactly what it was about him that made me love him, but I was smitten.

The hardest thing for me to grasp about Mr. Rob was how he had pointedly decided that there was no God. Not that I knew much about what people believed, but growing up in the South, it seemed unheard of to me for someone to openly denounce God.

Mr. Rob seemed so spiritual to me. His being was so alive. It didn't make sense to me. When you're little, in the South, you're not taught that there is anything but the people who believed in God, and that the people who didn't were surely going to hell. I, of course, never believed that Mr. Rob was going to hell, and if he was, I wanted to go there with him. Still, the news was shocking for a child with no exposure. It would be years before I understood that there was no hell, especially for Mr. Rob.

Mr. Rob's wife had died two weeks after the house on the canal was finished. The two of them were retiring to the little river community and the house on the canal. Mr. Rob's wife never got to live at their newly built retirement home; she spent the last weeks of her life in the hospital. Mr. Rob said he would never believe in a God that would take his wife like that, just before they were to share their most cherished time together. He was openly lonely without her; most of our conversations were about her. I wished every moment that I was with him that she was there too.

Everyone told my father that I was this great kid, never a problem, and that they loved to see me coming. I heard him brag about this. Looking back now, I see how it was, in a truer sense. I was the kid who was beaten into submission and careful observance of others by my mother. I'd not been allowed to be around other children, so I acted like the adults around me in this different environment. They were my only models, and I followed a strict, quiet decorum.

I'd bike the miles up and down the main road. There were no children on the major marina road but me. I played alone, which was what I'd preferred anyway. I explored the world, and took a break inside of myself from the constant fear and anxiety that I felt in my mother's house.

4

GONE WITH THE WIND

Claire, Dad's wife, was nice in the beginning, but she had some peculiarities that I couldn't help being aware of. One was that I'd not on many occasions seen her without a drink. For a beautiful woman, I found her soon to not be so beautiful. Eventually her eyes were different. They had a deep redness that didn't look right with her pretty olive skin color. She was still slow and graceful, but as time went by, she became sloppy.

At first, Claire would talk to me. She made sure I was set up comfortably in the room next to hers and my father's. She was sweet most days in the beginning, like she was afraid to say something that would confuse me, but something wasn't right about her.

I came in once, and she was watching "Gone with the Wind" and repeating the line, "Frankly, my dear, I don't give a damn," to herself, over and over again, in the dark, while holding a drink close to her lips. She knew I was in the room, but that didn't stop her.

She was lying on the couch in the tiny living area. I came in the door at her back. When she decided to acknowledge me, she told me that my dinner was in the kitchen and to go to my bedroom for the night when I was through. I did as I was told.

I was so oblivious at first about Claire, because I was so busy in my head being at peace for a bit from being away from my mother. I didn't think that much about Claire's behaviors, because I didn't want to get involved with her behaviors. If she didn't hurt me too much, I'd just get along. I knew that was my nature.

My father would come in from work on his workdays, make his rounds with friends, and take us out on the pontoon boat he had at the time. Life with him was easy.

I did notice that Claire's drinking seemed to be getting worse.

At one point I walked in from my bedroom to see my father taking a drink out of her hand. I was too young to understand that he must have been disappointed. He had, originally, adored Claire, but only in the novelty way that he did with new women. I think he had hoped his feelings for her would last.

Then one late afternoon before my father got home, Claire locked the door and wouldn't let me in.

"You stay outside and you're not coming in until I say so. I don't want to see you." She slurred her words and gnashed her teeth. Her eyes were red and mean. I could feel her fumbling with the lock, having trouble grasping the concept of turning it.

"Yes, ma'am," I stammered through the glass, not knowing what else to do. I just sat down on the high steps and daydreamed, wishing the Rays were home so that I could visit. I didn't want to go too far away. Dad worked late on some days with his policeman's schedule. I knew I was supposed to be in the house by sunset, though. When my father drove home, even well after dark, Claire let me in the house before he could see me sitting on the steps outside, waiting to be let in.

With Claire, different days brought different situations.

"I'll be home at four today, when you're out of school. Don't come home. I want to be alone." She glared at me and had trouble standing straight. She always seemed to stumble now. Her breath would take anyone back. "Yes, ma'am," was all I knew to say.

I never told my father, not even when she made me sit in the dark outside until nine at night on a school night. Why didn't I just tell him? I don't know. I just sat on those steps at the house on stilts waiting until she would let me in to go to bed. I was locked out of the house, and I was afraid I'd get in trouble with my father if I left the steps. Soon I was spending every early evening locked out of the house.

Then one morning I found an expensive gold necklace in the nightstand by my bed. I knew it wasn't mine, so I put it in Claire's jewelry box when she went in the bathroom to brush her hair. My father came home and she met him in the hall, furious. She was mumbling something that was clearly about me, but I just turned back to my room.

She called me into their bedroom. My father was sitting on the edge of their bed. "Lizzy, have you been in my jewelry box? I'm missing my favorite gold necklace, and I won't have you going in my things." She was ugly and mean. Holding her cup of coffee tightly, she wobbled to her jewelry box on the dresser, and looked stunned when she found the necklace that she had put in my nightstand at some point in the night.

"Isn't that your necklace, Claire?" my father looked relieved. "Lizzy, are you messing with Claire's personal things?"

"No, sir," I stared directly into his face. I was sad. I didn't know what to do about the way grownups made things look.

"Well, see that you're respectful of Claire's things, please. Meet me downstairs; we'll take the boat out this morning." I left, and as I left I heard her mumbling angrily to him about me. I didn't understand what was happening, but I just pretended it wasn't happening when it wasn't in my face directly. It's not like I was ever given the option to oppose anything, anyway.

Finally she just told me directly that I wasn't supposed to ever come in until nine when she was home. I paced the deck and steps in the dark until she unlocked the door. I wasn't allowed to live in her presence at all, in the house. I'd have to come in, grab a sandwich, shower, go to my room, lights out in a flash. I literally had only so many minutes to see that I got everything done. She would come in, and turn the light off in the room, even as I was trying to put my gown on, or finishing a sandwich that I wasn't allowed to eat in the kitchen or dining room. She said I wasn't quick enough and that I'd better go to bed and be asleep, right away.

"Your father's night shift is over tonight. He's going to be here in the evening for a while; you had better stay out of our way." She would say this while wobbling on her feet. She had a habit of getting right into my face with her liquored breath. This was now life with Claire.

I didn't think about her until I had to go home for the day. I loved my life on the river. Claire didn't know it, but she was nothing compared to the mother I'd come from. I bet she wondered why I never talked back and never reacted to her. I can imagine it was puzzling. She tried to push me in a variety of ways.

One day my father decided that I would go and spend a weekend in town with my sister. He made it like it was no big deal, just a visit.

When I was at my sister's, she sat me down and said she wanted to talk to me about Claire. I was fine with that, but I didn't know why.

"Lizzy, you've got to be better to Claire!"

"Okay," I said absently.

"Lizzy, are you hearing me?" she seemed astonished. "You can't treat her badly; you've got to be better."

"I try to stay out like she wants me to. I don't come in until nine." Leslie was on the couch. I was on my knees in front of the coffee table in front of the couch.

"What?" my sister was confused. I could see it in her face.

"I try to be invisible. I eat and shower as quickly as I can. I'm not fast enough." I was telling my sister what I understood. I didn't notice even that it was not okay, what Claire was doing to me.

"Lizzy, what do you mean, you don't come in until nine?" My sister, who was then twenty-three, and very protective of me, looked pale.

"She likes for me to stay outside until nine, after dark, but Daddy says I have to be at home before dark, around six. So I just hang around on the deck until she lets me in."

Leslie didn't say anything for a few moments.

"Lizzy, do you touch Claire's personal things?"

"No, but I've found some of her things in my room and put them away." I explained about the necklace, but at that time I just didn't see what my sister was so obviously seeing. My sister was realizing that Claire was lying to my father and mistreating me. I just saw that I survived grownups, and seemed to have fared well in this situation. Claire wasn't beating me, and I still got to live with my father on the river.

We didn't discuss it like you might think; my sister babied me to some degree. She was upset, I think, that I didn't grasp what was happening to me enough to tell anyone, and I could see that she despised Claire. I didn't, at twelve, fully grasp anything that adults did.

I spent more and more weekends with my sister, until her husband was angry that I was always there. I was at the dinner table with her and her husband one night when he came in for his dinner. He sat down, asked me to take my elbows off the table, then slammed his drink down and walked out the door. There was no way for my sister to protect me from the fact that her husband didn't want me there anymore.

"Don't worry about it, Lizzy. I love you. He's stupid!" If it makes any difference, she left him shortly after those days. He did not know how to be good to my sister. He was critical of her in every way. I saw it myself. I do think he was sorry though, when she left.

Since I wasn't able to go to my sister's, my father let me know that I would have to go back to my mother's.

"Lizzy, if you stay, I lose her. If you go, I lose you. I can't win and I have to live with Claire."

"Yes, sir," I said.

I turned away from him to hide my obvious hurt, fear, and pain. I went to my room and cried for a very long time. I did have feelings about returning to my mother's house. He and Claire made me come out for dinner, but I couldn't eat.

"Eat your dinner, Lizzy!" Claire said so hatefully.

"Yes, ma'am," I said. All I thought was, "Oh my God, I have to go back to my mother! What would she do to me after all of this?" I was afraid for good reason. I knew my father felt horrible, but I was learning that I was always on my own. I couldn't even look at him, and he couldn't look at me.

During the week that I was packing up, my father and Claire weren't around much. When Claire was there, she just kind of smiled sideways as she drank, and mumbled to herself. I didn't think much about it. I was consumed with fear of what was going to happen to me back at my mother's.

I did hear, later in life, that Claire ended up being quite an alcoholic. This was the talk; there's no way I could ever know what was really going on in those days. No one ever told me anything directly, either. I can only be speculative, with no facts in this case. I heard that she eventually lost her job at the investment agency, and that it had been a high position with the investment group. Whatever it was, my father was very proud of her in the beginning.

I didn't know that my father would very shortly divorce the very disturbed Claire. He met, around that time, the woman that he's still married to today, Chelsea.

My final morning of getting to live with my beloved father on the river, I accepted that I would have to go back into my mother's life. Other people would have looked at it all and said, "You're almost thirteen; in five years you'll be eighteen," but nobody knew that nothing, not even legal age, could save me from my mother.

My mother would find a way to end my life before I was eighteen.

She'd even threatened me many times with ruining me by putting me into an institution. She used to brag that all she had to do was have two signatures to put me away, and she always had two signatures. She had life; she had choices. I had the choice to go away in my head or not, to try to find some idea of peace within myself, until my time on earth was done.

That last morning I went through my albums to play a song while I waited for my father to pick me up and take me to my mother's. When I took the first record that I'd wanted to listen to out of its jacket, I realized that one of Claire's records was in my record's sleeve. I didn't know what had happened. I was confused for a moment, but then I went through each of my albums and found that Claire had actually replaced all of my records with her records. Even though I'd figured out what Claire had done, I didn't want to believe something so completely bizarre could happen. I felt hot all over, panicked by her behavior.

I was horrified as I rushed through the album sleeves, removing all of hers. I needed to take them to her albums and get mine out of her cases, and for the first time it hit me, the truth, that someone would purposely make you look in a way that wasn't what you were. She would make it look to my father like I was stealing her stuff. I felt like I was going to be sick.

I know I should have learned what people were capable of with my mother and that life with my mother, but when you're young, you're just mainly confused about what's wrong with you. It's hard to decide that someone else has something wrong with them. It just doesn't feel right. When you're a child, it's inconceivable to you that people can be bad that are around you, but you can certainly believe that you, yourself, are bad. If I hadn't caught what Claire had done, she would have had my father confront me and he would've had no choice but to believe that I had taken her albums.

I never told anyone about the records, not even Leslie. I was sick about it, and I didn't want anyone to know what had happened to me. I felt like something was terribly wrong with me that someone would feel like they had to go to such trouble to make trouble for me.

Sometimes I wonder, though, what it was like for Claire when she found that I had put her records back in their proper cases. Was she disappointed?

5

BACK HOME WITH MOTHER

Going back to my mother's was one of the hardest things I'd ever have to do. I didn't hate my father for taking me back to my mother's; maybe I understood that his wanting me was negotiable. Maybe that's how I measured my own existence. I was the expendable one.

My father did hate himself for it, though, for allowing me to go back to my mother, and it showed through the years in his staying further away, and when we were together he seemed washed with shame and distance. He was handicapped in his feelings towards me. He loved me, but he could no longer look directly at me for very long.

The confused love I had with my father made me not want to love at all, I think, not in a voiced, out loud way, so I spent my life avoiding love, unintentionally. Even though my mother had already taught me to be leery about people who were close to me, the thing with my father was different.

Mother was waiting for me, when my father and I walked up the steps to Mother's front door. He was deliberate with his steps. She owned him and she owned me in that moment.

"Lizzy, I'm glad you're home. I've missed you terribly." Her voice came out clear and kind. I believe she did miss me, but I couldn't tell what for. I just nodded in her direction.

Dad sat for a minute, and talked to her about nonsensical things. Then he stood up, to leave me with her forever. I remember always feeling bad for him and his feelings; I didn't know how to examine what my own feelings were, or to feel bad for myself. I was just sad to have to go back to a life where I had to be watchful and aware at all times.

Since Jessie was out of the picture, there was no welcoming party. The world just looked like this bleak waiting place, but I didn't know what I was waiting for. The family that surrounded me had convinced me that I had no value. I know that happens to many children. It wasn't something that was new, or unique, to me.

People say, "Aren't you happy? Aren't you proud? You've overcome so much in your life. You survived your mother!"

I say, "Yes, I'm proud." This is the response I give, but I'm caught up in confusion. I don't know what the goals are in this life. No one told me what our time here was for, and I don't know what I'm doing here. And, most important is the fact that I never lost the feeling of needing to survive. I haven't been able to teach myself out of survival, for all the counseling in the world.

My counselor would say, "You're safe, here, you're safe!" And I would have a seat near the glass doors, with my back to the wall, with one eye on the other door, and nod with what I wanted to appear as belief. I've always, consciously, guarded my parameters.

So, I went back, that day, back to the little brown paneled room down the hall, and it seemed, somehow, smaller. It was a tired room that knew me, in my habit of giving objects life in my mind.

"Hi, Lizzy, glad you're home, your green blanket's here, she didn't take it!" This was running through my mind, because I made sure my mother never knew that I loved the green bed blanket that I'd always slept with. After Carrot, my favorite stuffed toy, was taken, and Gretchen was thrown away, I'd finally learned.

The windows in that room were my eyes to the world for so long that I'd swear to you with my last breath that I loved those windows like they were family. Those paneled walls even, the way the closet doors slid just so, they were a part of me. I felt them intensely, not with love that made me be okay with being back there, of course, but with love that meant I would remember and live with them all the days of my life in panoramic view, somewhere, in the back of my mind.

The paneled walls of my bedroom knew all the parts of Lizzy that I had lost, and they must be regarded in my soul, in the highest, for that reason. I can still hear the eerie, "Hello, Lizzy," from some far off place that I'd imagined into existence.

I was sad, broken, and destroyed, as I laid my stuff down like someone who'd been grabbed by a giant and shaken dumb. This room was my institution, and at thirteen, my straightjacket was put back on, and the room greeted me like we'd never be apart again.

I could hear my mother talking to someone on the phone.

She yelled out to me, "Lizzy, get my cigarettes." She didn't seem mean yet, but I ignored her just the same. For some reason I wouldn't worry about her anymore. Maybe it had something to do with having nothing to lose.

While Mother was calling me, I examined everything around me more closely. The distance down the hall had been shorter to get to that place, the room, where I hid for so many years. The closet in the room was friendly, inviting, and the linen closet, as I tugged at the door in the hall, was so much smaller in my mind than it had been before.

"I missed you, Lizzy," I say in my heart and hear in my mind.

I remember wandering through that day at my mother's, and knowing, finally, that I would wander there and everywhere through all of time. I was okay with wandering, or I was resigned to it. I didn't know back then that all that was happening to me would someday be something that would make my life journey such a positive, moving, worth it all, kind of thing.

As a child, and that day at thirteen, I didn't wish to be someone else. I wasn't jealous of anyone else's experience. I just wanted to not be hurt, and I wanted to feel calm, because I'd not had a lot of that. I had no regret, and in my adult life I have no regret. The truth will always be that the life I lived with my mother made me see the world differently than most people do. I got the gift of my soul's eyes being opened early on in the game. I got to live, awake, I would say. My life has been fuller, because of my mother. I've lived many lives, in my head and otherwise, because of her. I will always feel gratitude for that.

DOWN SOUTH

1

GOING DOWN SOUTH

I sat with the windows down, in the humid Florida heat. Every breath I took felt like I was sucking hard, and the release of air wasn't that comfortable. I had on cutoff jean shorts and a blue t-shirt, and my knobby knees were scarred, streaked with adventure, streaked with my courageous heart.

I sat listening to my biological mother, Kay's, husband Rhett, talking to her about what they needed at a local auto part store, to get their too old car running again. I didn't know, at six, that this would be the theme of the six summers that I would spend with Kay and Rhett. All of their cars would always break down, forever and ever, amen.

I was adopted by Kay's sister, Susan, because Kay was a teenager who was "too young to pull it all together," by which, I guess, they meant too young to be a mother to me. That's the story anyway. Kay seemed nice enough. Rhett just loved old cars and read war history all of the time.

"You're going to spend the summer with Kay and Rhett in South Florida," Mother said between puffs of smoke. I didn't say anything; you just didn't say anything; that's the way it was. I had no idea what it would mean to visit Kay and Rhett for the summer.

"I stole you from her when you were sixteen months old. She left you at your uncle's house, and I took you home with me. Your dad didn't even know I was bringing a baby home. I let Kay know through the grapevine that she better not come around here trying to get you!"

I didn't respond. She didn't want or need a response, I had learned.

She just said things out loud to herself, between puffs of smoke. I didn't have feelings about going down South. As children, we just did what we were told. We were at the mercy of big people.

As the car moved down South, it felt wonderful to have the wind against my face. I listened to Kay and Rhett talk. Kay generally listened to Rhett, followed his lead in conversation, and if she didn't, if she expressed a feeling of her own, he got a little too excited that she felt differently than he did. He would then berate her into his way of thinking.

"I thought Susan was fine this trip. I'm happy to have Elizabeth for the summer." She would have hesitance in her voice as she waited for his dominance. Kay always called me Elizabeth, because she said that was the name she had given me at birth, not Lizzy. She was defiant about that point.

"She wasn't fine! Your sister's the worst bitch I've ever met in my life," Rhett was adamant that this was the case.

Kay tried to shush his language in front of me.

"Don't shush me, I don't like your sister and I don't care who knows it! She's a crazy bitch!"

I just watched and listened to the both of them. Kay was heavy, but shapely, with dark hair straight down her back. Kay was very short. Rhett was a male of average height, and his hair was a mix of brown with reddish copper tones.

"Why are you so fucking nice?" Rhett would wail out at her. Kay would then fall silent, until he let her know that he wanted to communicate with her again.

Rhett wasn't harmful or anything to me. He was completely wrapped up in Kay, and they were young. They were at that time in relationships where people generally are wrapped up in each other. I think of it now as that time when people are deciding who's the pack leader.

The singlewide trailer they owned in South Florida was powder blue. The inside was cluttered with things, boxes, old newspapers, sacks of clothes. There was a hole chewed into the kitchen floor by what Rhett called the skivvy cat. Rhett said the skivvy cat came in at night and that he'd killed one before, but you really had to clear out when you killed one, because of the smell.

I was six. I wasn't raised to see the fact that they lived in extreme filth. I just wanted to see the skivvy cat in real life. The trailer was full of wildlife; roaches had taken to living in drawers in hordes. If you opened a drawer, they scattered onto the counter. Kay used to spray bug spray all over the trailer. I remember breathing the spray in; in childhood I didn't understand that this wasn't healthy, and that I should avoid the spray. There was no way to escape it, though. The bug spray was everywhere.

The trailer had one room at the end of it, and a smaller room at the other end of it. The middle of the trailer was a living room and kitchen. The trailer reminded me of a shoe box, and in a storm, the tinny sound the rain made was remarkable.

The place was so full of clutter that I wasn't allowed to sleep in the smaller end room; I had to sleep in a folding metal lawn chair, beside the double bed in Kay and Rhett's small room. It was the kind of chair that people take to the beach in summer with the million fraying plastic strands. I didn't know to care about that. It seemed fine to me.

I also had to sleep in their room because it was the only room in the trailer that had air conditioning, a small window unit. If you've ever been down South, in the summer, you'd understand that you can't live without air conditioning. The tin trailer was so stifling hot that it was hard to breathe. The trailer material turned the trailer into an oven on wheels.

Kay must have told me twenty times a day: "Don't tell Susan about the skivvy cat, don't tell Susan about the mess we live in, don't tell Susan that you sleep in our room!"

'Don't tell Susan' was central to Kay, but I didn't know that Kay's life was bad until she told me it was.

We never ate at the trailer. I think once Kay tried to cook salmon patties in this electric pan that you could plug into the wall. Kay and Rhett ate pizza, and burgers, and then, pizza, and burgers again.

The first trips down South didn't have much of an impact on me. I was physically uncomfortable with the heat that seemed worse further south than it did on the upper panhandle, but I was an adaptable kid. I was told what to do and I did it. I wasn't excited or not excited about going. I wasn't taught to be connected to the idea of an opinion. Maybe most kids weren't, in those days.

Kay always worked in some Daycare. She was actually very good at that and well trusted with the lives of children. We were up at six taking Rhett to his construction site and heading to the Day Care. I think at least once every two weeks whatever car we were in would break down. Life was very hard for them. Every single day they woke up putting water in the car engine, hoping that it would get them through another day.

I remember the tired look on Kay's face. I remember the weaknesses I knew were hers right from the start of our acquaintance. I wasn't sad for her. I don't think I respected her. I didn't not like her, though, because she was kind to me and everyone else she came in contact with. Kay assumed the world knew more than she did on every subject. She even acted like I was smarter than she was, and I was a child.

On one trip, I tried to get her excited about cleaning up her trailer, unpacking various boxes, even washing dishes; she was always saying how she just wanted a real home. But she wouldn't even try. I remember there being no water, at some point, which happened periodically. I took dishes out to this spigot that worked in the yard to try to make some order, but she just wouldn't follow my example, or do anything for herself.

Those first few summers, Rhett hardly spoke to me, but he wasn't unkind to me. Kay was just self-conscious. Kay wanted to be my mother, but Kay didn't know how to be a person. I guess that's the trouble with a lot of people.

2

HIGH ON THE MOUNTAIN OF LOVE

The year that I was nine, Rhett and Kay had a baby, a son. When my half brother, Seth, came, Rhett was beyond himself with pride. He loved his new baby boy, as he should have. He and Kay had tried for many years to have a child of their own. When I went down south that particular summer, Rhett was completely wrapped up in Seth and so was Kay. I was thrilled to have adult attention some place other than on me, not that the two of them bothered me.

But then Rhett changed toward me in that summer after Seth was born. He had little patience for my presence in their lives. Kay wanted me there with them; it's probably the only thing in her life that she ever stood up for. Kay was consumed with the fact that I was taken from her as an infant, sixteen months old. She apologized to me every time I'd ever see her.

We, all four of us, lived now in a different shoebox trailer on the same land, with the powder blue trailer pulled back further on the land. I remember learning to hide from Rhett in the blue trailer. He wanted to think of the three of them as a family.

The new shoebox was looking like the last trailer pretty quickly, minus the skivvy cat. I remember the way Rhett and Kay slept until one in the afternoon on weekends all those summers. I'd have to find something to do to pass the time, which wasn't abnormal in itself. That's what kids do; we learned to pass the time.

The greatest thing I did in those long mornings was to learn to sing Johnny Rivers' "Mountain of Love" by heart. I loved an old Rivers album that I'd found in one of the many boxes tossed around the house. This was life, for some kids anyway. Our lives were small, quiet adventures. Sometimes they were good; sometimes they were not.

Sometimes we would visit Rhett's family. He had a brother, called Uncle Davis, that I adored secretly in my brain. He was tall, quiet, intelligent, gentle mannered, and the list could go on forever. He was such a gentleman, and even as a child, I did notice that.

Uncle Davis had a big gray house in the country, with a confusing, and seemingly unkind, wife attached to the deal. She was never unkind to me, though. She always spoke to me like I was an alive being. She just had a different sort of reserve about her. Maybe she was just misunderstood. Uncle Davis and his wife had two children, Kathy and Daniel; they were my age, with Daniel a few years older and very nice.

Kathy and Daniel's mother did not appear maternal. She was in her own world most of the time. As for Uncle Davis, he would be the beginnings of my first older male crushes. I hardly ever spoke to him, but his saying, "Hey there, lovely girl," with his bright, sensitive, open smile, made my little heart feel something like a warm flip.

I played with Kathy and Daniel, and loved the days we would spend there in the country. As I got older, Daniel's vulnerable eyes, tender height, and wet compassionate lips did not escape my notice. He would grow into his father for sure. Kathy was different. Where Daniel was soft and sensitive, Kathy was the fun party girl. I grew to love both people very much.

That summer that I was turning ten, we spent lots of time at my Uncle Davis's, and I played for hours with Kathy and Daniel.

Daniel and I had a connection, though, that still brings me quiet when I think about it. There was something in knowing him that moved me, and I didn't understand then that it was simply that Daniel was just so good and pure to me. He was a younger version of why I loved Uncle Davis.

Kathy, Daniel, and I played all over the cow fields that surrounded the big gray house. I have this memory of Daniel, very nerdy, with his thick black glasses gazing out a window of this old bus that we played in at the far end of one of the pastures. He was holding on to a ridge in the roof of the bus. With the weight of his body in his hands, he hung forward in front of me, just so. Kathy was with her mother somewhere that day. I could hear the sounds of trees hitting the side of the bus. I remember the color of the blue in the sky.

Daniel turned his eyes to me ever so slowly. His head was tilted low, and his green eyed gaze was coming from the top of his thick black glasses. I just walked right up to that look, and with true fear and confusion, I felt that warmth in his eyes. My face was only a few inches from his, maybe. I didn't know what to do with whatever I was feeling for him. My body was nearing his. I could see it in his eyes that he was nearing me. We just had that thing, in the air, that you don't know what to do with yet. I could move close to him because he would never have pursued me.

The warm encounters with Daniel were always in my mind as the summer went on. Soon our faces were centimeters apart, then touching just so, mouth to mouth, without our bodies ever touching. There was this funny way he let his arms fall, like he was letting me know that he wouldn't touch me. These were quiet moments that no one saw.

I was scared to get too near Daniel, but there were times when I allowed it to happen. I had some sick feelings and self loathing that I understand now to be from the sexual abuse that I'd experienced. I would be compelled to feel the warmth of being near Daniel's face, brushing my cheek against his mouth, until our lips met, but then I would feel so sick to my stomach that I would go seek out Kathy, wherever she had gone.

Daniel was kind, always. I'm awfully sorry that I must have been confusing for him. I will always appreciate the way that he could look at me and really see me.

Age doesn't mean much in reality. I learned that early on. Exposure to yourself, to life, is what awakens us in good ways and in bad in the journey. I never felt ten years old. I never felt four. I just felt endurance, information, and my existence in time.

Life had a different structure for me, after the worst abuse from Al. I was edgy, sick a lot. I had worries, imaginary and real, at every turn. And then I started having to worry about Rhett.

Kay made me take showers at the same time she did in the trailer, because of a water issue. I don't know why, but the water had to be turned on outside before our showers, and our showers had to be quick. Kay made me be undressed in the bathroom, waiting for her to get out of the shower. The door was open into the pitch black hall. I remember turning around in utter confusion. Kay wouldn't let us shut the bathroom door for some reason I didn't understand. I felt vulnerable, unsafe in an ever-enduring way I couldn't escape from. When I turned near the door, I realized that Rhett was standing in the hall watching me naked.

"Rhett!" I jumped and grabbed my towel. He just looked coldly into my eyes and walked away back down the dark hall.

"Kay, Rhett was just there! Maybe we should hurry!" I trembled all over waiting for her to give me a turn to shower. There was no hot water and I just kept trembling.

I slept in the same room with the crib and the two of them. The only air conditioner in the house was in the one room. It had always been that way. I woke up one morning because of the noise they were making in the bed next to me. I was confused, and afraid to move on my nylon beach lounge chair. I sat up and Rhett was on top of Kay with me in the room. I just lay down quickly and acted like I didn't see anything, that I'd fallen back asleep. I was young, so I didn't understand how mistakes like that could be made. I was too young to compute that Kay was possibly letting it happen because Rhett wanted me to see them.

"Don't tell Susan what Rhett was doing at the bathroom door," Kay instructed me. Her voice was harsher than usual.

"Yes ma'am," my only response.

"Don't tell Susan what you saw this morning!"

"Yes, ma'am."

I was so glad when I was about to leave that summer. I knew Rhett was working his way toward me, and Kay wasn't strong enough to stop him. She was also giving me the, 'Don't tell Susan,' thing. I never told the Mother anything anyway, but my hands were always tied when a grownup told me what I should do. I didn't know how to go against anyone.

Kay was so angry that she could see that I was visibly happy to be leaving. She kept saying things like, "I hope you're not like Susan. I sure hope you're not hard-hearted like her, because that's what I'm seeing." Her normally submissive face was changing in time to something resentful of me.

3

RHETT

I went down South for the last time the next summer when I was eleven, turning twelve. Kay and Rhett were apartment sitting for the summer for one of the mothers who brought her children to the Daycare where Kay worked.

I didn't mind going to the Daycare this particular summer. I knew it from the summer before, and the kids seemed to like me there. The only bad part was that Kay sent me to this hamburger place most days for her lunch, and the hamburger place was too far away to walk to for anyone, much less for a young girl walking by herself. I had to cut through yards and walk on a major highway to get there. I was afraid of getting lost, kidnapped, or killed.

On my way to the hamburger place I was always concerned about the yards I would have to go through, and what people would do if they caught me trespassing. I was actually afraid of any male encounter that could possibly occur. I was grateful each day when I got back to the Daycare and handed the lunch over to Kay.

Kay was fine this particular summer. She liked being in the apartment instead of the dilapidated trailer.

As for me, I had started the visit half out of my mind because of how Rhett had started behaving at the end of the previous summer. I was filled with worries about Rhett, and wondering how I could keep him off of me. In my experience, men didn't stop because of any time lapse. They would just keep moving in for the kill.

Soon after I arrived this last summer, I would walk into a room and find Rhett masturbating there. At first I was confused. There was a window opening between the kitchen area and the living room area. It was a small apartment; you could see everything in the living room from the opening. Kay would go to the store. I'd turn to go get dishes off the kitchen table, and Rhett would be sitting, masturbating, in plain sight, in an arm chair in the living room.

The first time he did it, I just bolted around, and acted like I didn't see what he was doing. I was frantic. I knew he was going to do what Al did, and I didn't want to live that again. I couldn't tell anyone. There was no one to tell. I was shaking all over. I remember the dishes clattering in my trembling hands.

The next time it happened, on another day, I had turned to tell him something without paying attention to what he was doing. When he didn't answer the question I asked, I realized that he was doing it again. My body jolted backwards when my eyes fell down on what he was doing. I remember the look in his eyes before my eyes fell low; he looked defiant, even angry toward me. I couldn't make out what was happening.

When Kay would come back in, he would be cool to her, and act like nothing had happened. I remember her asking me once what the matter was with me when she got home from some errand, because I was visibly trembling. I heard her go in and ask Rhett what was wrong with me, but I think he ignored her. They both went to bed.

I don't remember how many times Rhett did that. He seemed to be meaner to me every day, acting like I wasn't in a room, and then, when no one was around, he would make sure I had to see him masturbating.

Finally, I was lying in my small bedroom one night, waiting for the door knob to turn. I knew Rhett was coming. I just didn't know when. Sometimes the door knob would turn and it would be Kay telling me something, but I knew eventually it would be Rhett.

When he came into the room, my body tightened up all over. I remember the physical trembling of my person.

"Lizzy, come out. Let's go in the living room." His voice had the false kindness in it that I had heard him use with strangers.

"No, no, I'm just about asleep. Good night, Rhett." I drew the sheet tighter around me.

"No, come on out to the living room."

"I'm really tired Rhett, I was almost asleep," I tried again.

He came up to me, sat on the edge of the bed, pulled the covers back with a sweep, and demanded that I come out to the living room.

He was still using the fake nice voice mixed with his angry, 'you'd better come now,' voice.

When I reached the living room, I saw that blankets were laid out like a bed made on the floor. The carpet underneath had been a dark rust color.

"Lay down, Lizzy."

"I want to go back to my room, Rhett. I'm very tired." I was trembling, and trying to act natural at the same time. I was trying to protect myself. He seemed to be enjoying the methodical things that he had started doing to me that summer. He acted like there were no consequences for what he was doing, and I guess there weren't.

"Lay, down, Lizzy! Now!" He wasn't going to let me go, but I hadn't given up on getting away yet. I lowered my body slowly to the blankets and pillows.

He lay next to me and pulled a sheet over us. He got right in my face. He was still in his shorts and a t-shirt. I was still in my pajamas. He was revolting. There was only a dim light in the living room coming from the stove light in the kitchen.

"I want to teach you to kiss," he said in a low voice.

I panicked, "No, I don't want to kiss, I already know how."

"No, there's a special way to kiss that I want to teach you."

"Rhett, I already know how to kiss. Please let me go to bed." My heart was racing.

"Come on, you'll want to kiss me, it's special, more than just a quick peck."

Rhett was evil. His eyes were on me, his prey. I didn't count! I didn't matter! My life was of no importance to him. He wanted to get into my head. He wanted to take me away from myself. He wanted me to belong to him. I knew what that was about.

"Rhett, I know how to kiss. I don't want to kiss you that way." My body was rigid, drawn into myself. I thought I could feel my bones creaking from the tightness of squeezing myself inward.

"What do you mean? Who did you kiss that way, with your tongue in someone's mouth?" Rhett looked baffled. He was wondering what I knew at twelve years old.

"I've kissed that way, Rhett. I don't want to kiss you that way. Please let me go back to bed now. I don't want to do this."

I don't know why he let me go, but he did. I stumbled like an idiot to the room I was staying in. I lay staring at the ceiling all night waiting for Rhett to come in again, praying that he wouldn't. I was sweating, tense, and I didn't know what to do about this life, how to keep surviving it.

In the morning, I was waiting for Kay to get up so I could finally tell someone something that was happening to me. I was hoping so much that I wouldn't have to be this way with a man again.

"Rhett tried to teach me to kiss last night." I set all my fear aside at 6 o'clock in the morning.

"What, what do you mean?" she stammered. She was angry with me; I could see it in her eyes.

"Rhett tried to teach me to kiss last night. He brought me out here on a blanket while you were sleeping."

"What?" she seemed angrier as I repeated it, out loud, again. Her voice was like, how dare I say such a nasty thing, and say it again? It was like she was hoping my story would change in the air the second time around.

"Rhett makes it where I have to see him touch himself. He does things to himself in front of me!" I held firm. I didn't care about her, and whatever feelings she might have had. I was through with that at twelve.

Kay spun around, ran into the bedroom where he was, and I could hear her screaming at him, but what she was saying wasn't quite clear. She emerged from the room screaming at me, "How did you know what jacking off was? Where did you hear those words?"

I was stunned. I hadn't used those words and I told her I hadn't used those words. She spun around again to go back into where Rhett was.

Kay was weak. Her getting upset didn't really mean anything to him, anyone would know that. I think he was probably ignoring her.

She came into the kitchen, full of rage, and I would have sworn, for some odd reason, the rage was at me for telling her. I couldn't figure it out.

"Don't you ever..., in your life..., ever..., tell anyone about this! Do you hear me?" Her nostrils were flaring; she looked like she'd been caught at something. The scene was murky, strange. I just stared at her, evaluating her movements towards me.

"Not ever, do you hear me, Elizabeth?"

I still just stared at her.

"Elizabeth, men just do these kinds of things. You better never tell anyone!" She was being nasty to me! If she thought I was afraid of her, she was out of her mind, but I do believe that she thought she closed the subject.

Kay disgusted me. I never gave her an answer. This was the week that I was going back, and I was done with her. She was worthless in my eyes.

She made cruel remarks the whole week about how I was just like Susan, and how Susan had rubbed off on me.

This was the first time I'd ever told someone about an incident with a man to try and protect myself. It ended up not being worth much to tell anyone, when I tried.

4

KAY

"**B**ut, you know that I love you." Dolly Parton sang the song that would remind me of my knowing of Kay in the only positive way possible, forever. It was not the song that Kay chose and gave to me.

My biological mother, Kay, gave me Dolly Parton's record, "I Will Always Love You." It was from the movie The Best Little Whorehouse in Texas. The 45 had a picture of the whorehouse on the cover.

I didn't come from puritanical people. They never said they knew the way in life, and I will always value that. So it was completely fitting to get a picture of a whorehouse on the cover of a 45. There was no censorship in my family; there were no children anyway, just little people that age gave eventual rights to.

Kay gave me the record and told me that the song was my song from her.

"Every time you hear this song in your life, I want you to remember how much I love you, because, Elizabeth, I will always love you!" She stood before me, in her twenties, not yet broken down by the life she led. Her physical health was still intact. She had tears in her eyes. I remember being uncomfortable with her show of emotions. I hadn't been taught to cry. I hadn't been taught to feel. I took her tears as a part of her weakness, I'm sorry to say, even at that early age.

"Yes, ma'am," I'd say, while trying to figure out what facial expression to give her, to give her what response she needed from me. Kay was longing for something that I could never solve for her. I never knew what a natural response to any emotion in the world was, but she always expected something from me.

179

This was what Kay and I did: she stared into my eyes, eyes she could never know or understand, and watched for Susan, her evil sister to appear in them. She was in luck, because if you look long enough for something bad or evil in a person, you will always, inevitably, eventually find it, even if it comes in the form of a misunderstanding on your part, or an error in judgment on your part. All in all, we will see what we most need to see in order to keep ourselves safe from the ones we love. Kay wanted to be safe from loving me.

In Kay's honor, and against my will, I remembered her every time I heard Dolly Parton sing "I Will Always Love You," and then, when Whitney Houston sang it, and then, whenever the syllables were verbalized by anyone. I still, to this day, turn, in the stillest room, when I hear that song. Kay did that to me!

My life was always haunted by the conditional love Kay wanted to give me, but couldn't, because I, the real live human, was always in the way. I was haunted, caught in the middle of the two women who had inserted themselves into my life. I felt the fact that I was made up of the two of them, and I was. Their blood, their lives, coursed through my veins.

The psychological pressure Kay put on me was so great that I'll think about it in the quiet moments of my life forever.

"You're just like Susan," she screamed, when I was still young enough to be made to listen to her fears. That curse upon me from Kay has been profound. Did I not live enough of my life confused about Susan, and what my relationship with Susan meant to me?

"I can tell from the hardness in you, you're her, you're not me. No part of me is in you! I'm so sorry about who you are!" This was when I was eighteen, when she denied what Rhett had done to me, denied it to my heated face, in a very dark conversation in a night so deeply dark that it seems to spin into forever in my mind.

I hurt so badly for years because she had accused me of being Susan—from the moment I wouldn't allow Rhett to hurt me, from the moment that I saw what she was. She warned me about the possibility of being like Susan before I was eleven, but when I stood up for my own life, that was all it took to make me Susan completely. I looked at this woman, and my head ached and throbbed with reality. I couldn't believe people like her existed.

"Yes, I'm like her! I'm like Susan!"

"I know you are, I've seen it for so long now. Rhett says you're a walking, talking, Susan!" She glared at me, but she didn't see me, she wasn't capable of it. I sat at eighteen wondering what she wanted with me, if she couldn't even see me.

"I'm like Susan," I screamed back. "I got it...and I'd rather be her any day, than be the weak person that you are." My brain raced with fear and reality mixing, the fear that I could never show. Kay wasn't psychologically deep enough to understand me, while Susan was so psychologically deep that she'd use my fears to control me. There was no safe place between the two of them.

I am Susan, I thought. I'm certainly not a woman that would let a man sleep with her daughter. I'll be the evil one, I thought. I'll slip into the darkest side of myself, but I will never be a woman like you, Kay. I will never fall so deeply into a man that I'll give my daughter as a sacrifice to him!

With Susan's stories about my grandmother allowing her to be sexually abused, I have to think that Kay was used by my grandmother, too, that Kay as a girl had been given to men for sex. I can only speculate.

If Grandma made Kay have sex with men, too, then maybe Kay was doing with me what she was taught to do. Maybe in Kay's mind I was supposed to do sexual things with her husband, and pretend it wasn't happening. She never seemed to be a very smart woman.

In the last conversation I ever had with Kay before she died, after she had finally admitted what Rhett had done to me, and told me she didn't know why she had allowed that to happen, we had a different kind of conversation.

I started out: "I'm okay with the past now, Kay. I'm okay, relieved, I guess, just to have the truth. To not always be the person in exile, because of everyone else's lies, is something. I thank you, I do. What I don't get, though, is why, with men, with people, I guess, well, why don't they just say they're sorry? If people just said they were sorry, that would be something."

Kay was soft spoken, "I know." She seemed relieved at what I was saying, for some reason. "I know. I'd like that, too. If people would say they were sorry, that would mean a lot."

Now, I listen to Dolly sing, "You know that I love you!"—not the more famous, "I Will Always Love You." To me the famous song just hurts too much to hear. The loss in that song seems so final. The song, "You Know That I Love You" makes me think of Kay because the song talks about how a person has to travel away from someone they love and value, and how that's hard, but the love always exists anyway. The relationship in the song seems more ongoing.

Kay was a beautiful spirit, and it hurts me to know that she is gone. I know, now, that I was like her in so many ways. I know the good part of me, my sweetness, when I find it, comes from her, just like I know my conviction and my strength come from Susan.

Kay simply wanted the love of her siblings, and of me, her only daughter. Kay wanted to fit into a happiness that this life did not give her. Our family, in all its history, was dysfunctional. I look back on Kay as an Innocent, almost, in this life.

Sometimes I think, just maybe, that she chose the role she would play in this journey, before she came here, to do a small part towards getting better before returning home. I'm very sorry that she is lost to me now. The older I get, and the more I know myself, the closer I get to knowing her.

I'm sorry Kay, for it being too late for us to share any part of our lives together. I'm sorry most selfishly, for myself. When I think about you and about Susan, I feel like someone has knocked the wind out of me.

Your deaths were so final and frightening to me, that it scares the hell out of me some days when I wake up and find it still true, all over again.

FOUR
FAREWELLS

1

KAY'S DEATH

Eventually, when I got back from that summer with my relatives, I had to tell my mother about Rhett, so I wouldn't have to go down South again. I actually told Quentin, and he took care of it for me.

Kay had denied what Rhett did to me, as if it didn't happen. This action on her part made it where I could not be around her. Being around her felt dangerous for me.

When I was eighteen, Kay came to town to see everyone. She pleaded with me by phone to meet with her. She wanted a relationship with me, and I explained that I couldn't be around her husband after what he did to me, that Rhett frightened me.

I explained to her that I also couldn't be around a person who condoned a grown man telling a little girl he would teach her to kiss, and who allowed him to expose himself naked to me. I told her that I didn't believe that this was "just what men did." She became angry, hard, nasty, and indignant to me, and I told her that I had never been more ashamed in my life of being connected to another person.

Kay said she didn't remember me ever telling her that he was trying to teach me to kiss, or exposing himself to me. She added that she would never believe he could do such a thing, unless she saw it with her own eyes.

I felt then like any person does when they're faced with a bizarre unreality. I couldn't believe she would actually lie to my face, or support him and not me.

When I was in my twenties, Kay and Rhett moved up from South Florida. She moved into my mother, Susan's neighborhood, down the street. Kay wanted to live out her last years around her family and her daughter, and all but her daughter she did have until the end. I wasn't around Kay at all in my adult life, not having come to terms with what she had allowed Rhett to do to me in my younger days.

For years when Kay ran into me after she moved to town, she acted like the thing with her husband hadn't happened and instead begged me to forgive her for letting me be taken from her by Susan when I was a baby. She always wanted to talk about how my mother had stolen me from her.

This had been the theme of every time I saw her, since I was about seven years old. She had pleaded with me in anguish so many times to forgive her for letting Susan take me that I started taking a few minutes wherever we were to explain to her that she had to forgive herself for allowing me to be taken, that she had done the best she could do, and that she had to move on.

We could be standing in an aisle at a store, and all I wanted was for her to forgive herself and move on. She pleaded anyway, no matter how much I said I forgave her. She never heard me, all of our lives, and she never heard my voice, or my feelings, even once.

Kay had always regretted the loss, this painful early loss, which is to her credit. Not everyone can say that their absent parent actually tried to be with them throughout their lives. Of course it didn't mean much in the larger reality of our lives.

Kay was devastated a year or two before her death when I finally explained to her that, in the big picture, I had lived the lesser of two evils by being adopted by Susan. In essence, I could be Susan's daughter and taught how to be a survivor, or I could have been raised by her, Kay, and been raped my entire life by her husband while she cowardly looked away. Kay's face lost all color. She didn't know what to say.

I explained again to her that she should just let go of caring about Susan's taking me from her, and that I thought it was good that I wasn't forced into being her husband's second wife, trashed out, and turned into nothing, because of his sicknesses and hers.

In the end, before Kay's death, she called me and wanted to be a part of my life again. For the millionth time I explained to her that because she didn't accept what Rhett had done to me, she was a threat to me internally. I explained that I could have accepted meeting her, without him, occasionally for lunch or whatever, if she had just said she was sorry and that she knew what he did to me. But she wouldn't give me that, and it made her like everyone else who had hurt me in my life.

But this time, on the phone, she surprised me. She said, "Elizabeth, I don't know why I acted like he didn't do what he did to you. All I can tell you is that he was all I ever had. He was the only person that ever took care of me."

I held the phone away from my ear for a minute. The reality of Kay and her life washed over me. The reality of what it must have cost her to admit what her husband had done really knocked me back. I was relieved to have the truth said, because somehow it made me feel less invisible, but then I felt so bad for her.

I told Kay that I appreciated her calling and that I would talk to her soon, but her death was not long after. Just when I was really seeing her and what her difficulties and struggles were, she was gone. Just when I was finally losing my rage and fear, she slipped away from me.

Leslie called from the hospital. Quentin called from the hospital. All of Rhett's family was there at the hospital while she lay dying.

My mother, Susan, had taken a backseat to all current affairs; she had taken to her living room easy chair for years by then, waiting to die. She had been waiting to die since I was twelve and she had her first open heart surgery. All I ever heard from her was how she didn't have much time left, and all I thought, even as a girl, was, "If you're waiting to die, why not just end it all already, and free us all from your misery? We're all dying, for God's sake."

When Kay was dying, I was at a campground forty-five minutes away as my brother and sister were calling me from the hospital. I didn't answer my phone, but I did check my messages. It was not my intention to go to the hospital. Kay had lived her entire life, every time she ran into me, in anguish over the fact that she had let me go as an infant. I wanted to let her die in peace. I did not want Kay lying on her death bed apologizing to me.

In the end, I went to the hospital, against my judgment, because I felt pushed into it. In the middle of a horrific storm, I was at a stoplight looking at the gray and white hospital, when Quentin called to tell me it was over. She was already gone. I sat confused at the traffic light for a few seconds as the storm hurled itself around my car.

When I went inside the hospital, I was greeted by Quentin. He told me he would look out for me upstairs; he was expecting a lot of people's anger towards me for not being there at that weekend's vigil.

I told Quentin no, thank you, to the help. I said that they all made me who I was, and that I would face the room on my own.

Something in that moment, my attitude towards him maybe, made me see that I wasn't someone Quentin could know anymore. It's like you can almost hear the severing in the air when it goes on between people.

Up the elevator we went. I grew harder with every movement. My heart was hard, and my brain defied the pain and confusion. I wasn't going to let them hurt me anymore. I must have looked like a dark person when I reached the floor, because I looked up, and all I saw was Quentin's two children, whom I'd tried to be close to, and then Jessie. All three of them kind of bolted back, when they saw my face.

"Aunt Lizzy!" my niece said. She looked horrified. I felt myself jolt with what my face must have read. I hated that she saw my look of numbed-out controlled, but not controlled, rage.

"Lizzy, Lizzy, come here." His voice came softly from somewhere many years ago.

I just stared and felt his voice. I was ashamed of my face? Why was I so ashamed of my face? Why was I ashamed that I was showing my feelings of rage at all of them? I told myself that I had to be prepared for what they would do to me.

"Lizzy, come here." His voice was sharper, clearer, a voice I knew once. I turned to Jessie.

My eyes were steel rays. I felt like I was in a box and all these noises were banging around my box. I'd removed my mind from any blunder. I saw tears streaming down his face. It broke my heart.

I walked up to him.

He closed his arms around me, and I was grateful. Jessie was there, and just like when we were little, he knew how to feel and I didn't. My shame left me. I calmed down. He always calmed me down. I'll always remember that.

2

KAY'S FUNERAL

I stood in front of the full length mirror in my bedroom. I was running my hand down my stomach lightly. I was daydreaming, caught up in the fabric of the floor length black dress I was wearing. The room I stood in wasn't very bright, even though it was sunny out; I had the shades partly drawn.

I stepped closer and reached out to manipulate the mirror to an angle where I could see myself better. I decided to look at myself, which is something that I rarely ever do. I'm a small woman. I caught a lot of flak for that when moving into womanhood; the women in my family are robust.

My hair in adult life is generally kept long, and is a mix of brown and black. My mother kept my hair short when I was young because she said it would make it thicker when I was a woman. She said that a woman should not have short hair. My hair is very thick and heavy, and my mother thought it very beautiful, and praised her short haircuts for doing their job. It was the only compliment she ever gave me.

I'm five foot two, very short in the eyes of my family. I've always felt, because of the pressure that I was under my whole life, that at any moment I would completely evaporate into thin air.

I stepped away from the mirror. I was headed to Kay's funeral, where my family would be judging me, and I felt pretty tired, pretty bad.

I pulled into the funeral home parking lot, parked my car, and went and stood with my brothers. Leslie wasn't talking to me. She was mad because I had avoided the hospital vigil and because I avoided our family altogether.

Now, standing there with my brothers, I felt like I was being watched by all hundred or so people. I saw the eyes of Rhett's family and my family on me. I feel embarrassed to say that some people were fascinated by my appearance. It seemed that they thought I was pretty, or worldly, somehow.

People commented on my appearance a lot and seemed to take my hand lightly while telling me they were sorry for my loss. I couldn't tell what they were actually thinking. I was betting they were wondering why I came for the funeral if I'd refused to be a part of her life.

I walked up to the casket. My mother, Susan, was standing before Kay and telling me how good she looked lying there in her silky white and rose burial dress. It was more than I could bear.

I felt dizzy, and Mother went on to say how she hoped I would not treat her the way that I did Kay as she lay dying, because it must be understood that she didn't have much time left, she was sure of it!

I stepped away from the casket for a moment to let my mother finish saying goodbye to her sister and go. Then, as I stood there alone, I felt a presence behind me. The pews were filling, the room was crowded, but I knew the presence was one that wanted to actually be near me.

Rhett came up beside me and, though I usually went the other direction when I saw him coming, I just stood there. He couldn't hurt me anymore. I had nothing to be afraid of, and looking at him out of the corner of my eye, diminished, was hard for me, no matter what he had done. Rhett loved Kay, and loved her deeply. I was very sorry for his loss.

Both Rhett and I were shoulder to shoulder. He reached in to touch her, and said, "Lizzy, I sure hope I was a good husband to her."

I felt Rhett's pain and assured him that he had been a wonderful husband, that he had taken care of her all of her life, and that had been what she wanted. I think he appreciated my kindness. After all, he was the only one in the room who knew why I didn't have a relationship with my biological mother, but still, he would never apologize. He would have the world believe I was a bad person, and like Susan.

We all sat as Rhett's brother, Uncle Collin, got up to talk about Kay before all of the people. As he announced her survivors, one son, one daughter, and two grandchildren, who were my children, I froze and went completely weary. That was in the newspaper's announcement, too. I wasn't comfortable being announced as Kay's daughter. It tore me apart. These people didn't understand what had happened in my life. I never acknowledged her as a parent. The announcement was in no way true, and I had to live with the fact that she died in the way that she did. It was all pretty unbearable.

Uncle Collin sang a song, at Kay's request, but I was so numb that I don't remember it. The best thing was seeing Uncle Davis. As the funeral ended, he smiled at me so brightly from across the aisle. He was in the second set of pews directly beside me, and to my heart's joy he was in his dark grey mechanics clothes that he had worn on every other day of his life. I could see why I still had the biggest crush on him.

Uncle Davis was in his late sixties and coping with Alzheimer's. He took my arm in his. What luck for me to have such a man take my arm in my time of need, taking strides to say goodbye to Kay. Uncle Davis was tall and good looking, even in his sixties. His spirit was high, light, and brilliant.

When we reached the casket, he nudged me forward to give me an opportunity to speak to Kay lying there, but I just shook my head to let him know that I was okay and he could go on.

Uncle Davis looked at me like a child would, in a man's body. It moved me so. He then reached out while leaning over Kay's body. He grabbed her hand and announced as loud as loud could be, "Save a place for me now, honey!" He giggled to me and himself, and squeezed my arm a great deal tighter as he danced us out of the room.

I caught Jessie from the corner of my eye. He was looking hard at me. We were sharing a private moment of supportive hysteria, just like in the old days. It was a beautiful moment, Uncle Davis dancing me out. I'll always be grateful for what Uncle Davis gave to me in that moment. He did death right, God love him.

At grave side I talked to people I hadn't seen in years, people I had loved, especially Uncle Davis's two children, Kathy and Daniel. Daniel brought his wife and his new baby boy to the funeral. I think the baby was just under a year old; the baby was active, alive, and reminded me so much of his father. I couldn't resist playing with him. I remember Daniel saying in his loving, patient, observant way, "Well, look who's being spoiled." I remembered how sounds came softly from his mouth. I felt his careful eyes on me. His voice had always been like a whisper; his observance had always been keen. I'll always remember that.

Uncle Davis sat for a while with perfect, tall, rail thin posture, on a tomb. I sat with him for a little while. The cemetery was full of trees and natural splendor. The wind blew softly, but let its presence be known.

Uncle Davis wasn't always coherent with the conversation we were having, meaning that he tried to stay focused on whatever subject he wanted to talk about, but then his ideas would suddenly appear lost. I sensed some embarrassment from him in that. I put my arm around him, squeezed him tighter.

"Girl, you sure are a sweetheart, you always were. I'm sure gonna miss your mama." His voice was solid. His strong hands lay in his lap, as he swayed his knees side to side a little. He was kind of leaning over. The trees overhead must have loved him. All of life and existence must have loved him. I loved him.

"Yes sir, yes sir, I know you'll miss her." I leaned my head on his shoulder for a while.

Later, Jessie stood with me near the casket. Rhett was hanging around the grave. My half brother, Seth, whom I'd never had a relationship with, was doing the same. They were lost and didn't know what to do with themselves. I was leery of Rhett and I didn't know Seth that well; there was nothing I could do.

People came from down south who had had kids in Kay's Daycare. They kept coming up to me and saying they were sorry for my loss. Kay never told anyone that we didn't have a relationship. She asked me to hide that years ago, and I respected her wishes. I didn't know what to do. I felt ashamed that people kept acknowledging me as her daughter. I had not earned that.

At first I was unnerved by people walking up to me and saying, "I can't believe how much you look like your mother." People would walk up to me, stare into my face for long seconds, and then pronounce that I was just the identical image of Kay as they had known her in prior years. I knew that I looked like her, folks. I'd never been comfortable with that. I'd seen through the years when I'd get photos back from the photo shop that I'd slowly morphed into her. I had not trusted Kay in my life, so it was hard to see her in my own face.

I was kind to the people who took the time to speak with me

about Kay, and I eventually stopped flinching when they told me how much I looked like her. I knew the day belonged to Kay. I think I did fine. It did me good to see people who really loved and respected Kay, my mother.

Leaving the funeral, I passed Rhett who was examining headstones. He was a history buff, always reading all the time I knew him.

"Just like you, examining the dates," I explained, walking wearily by in the heat.

He smiled a little; he had always had a youthful smile. "Yeah, this one dates only a hundred and twenty years ago. Not too old."

I shrugged and laughed, "Take care of yourself, Rhett."

"Yes, you do the same. Thank you, Lizzy."

Then I trudged away, leaving Rhett far behind me, forever.

3

PAUL

Because I loved my father, I can't hear a certain song without breaking down inside. Some part of me comes undone, in the stillest, quietest center of my being.

I love him like love is, in its essence, in its purest form, in the way that little girls love their fathers. His stature is straight and true. I tried to make him innocent, but he was not, and consequently, he never asked to be.

He held my hand at a wedding he didn't approve of. He elegantly moved me over a dance floor in his way. He was charismatic, the world loved him, and he was in love with the world.

Women watched him… I watched him. I never understood that it wasn't a competition, not that I fought for my father's attention, but the women would come and go. I would always remain. Even if I wasn't a part of his life…I was the one called daughter, and nothing will ever be higher in life, in my eyes.

My counselor said that lots of people struggle with the unavailable charismatic parent. The world gets the wonderful person; the child does not. It isn't about handsome features. It's something else that a person has. It's an energy that lightens life and makes people happy. He was, in fact, very handsome, though.

My father sat in my living room a few evenings before I was to wed a very serious man. He took a seat in the middle of the room, and every woman I knew congregated around him, young and old. It was always the way of our lives. His neat gray cowboy hat was always just so. He wasn't a cowboy, but he was a Southern gentleman.

I watched the scene with adult eyes, holding my glass of wine, while wishing for hard liquor. I wasn't angry. I was stunned by time, and I was stunned by our unexamined lives. I always saw the world in panoramic stillness. Observing my father was no exception.

I was the little girl who acted too young, needing her daddy to be a daddy her whole life long, but the truth was, in this regard, I was like all the women who wanted to be the favorite in his eyes.

Maybe it was because I was adopted that I had fought so hard in my mind to know him, or maybe it's because I never got over the fact that he left us for something else.

I lived, in later life, tallying the points, discovering scores that weren't in my favor, guessing at what it all had meant anyway.

I have a picture, in my house, of that evening before the wedding, me holding my glass of wine, looking in the direction of the wildly beautiful man, surrounded by all the women of my acquaintance. He glittered; his voice lightened up and brought fun to an entire room.

I was stunning that night and I knew it. I was stunning in my wisdom, in my perception of who he was. The gift to myself that night was the fact that I'd acknowledged that I was on the inside of it all, that knowing of him. I did know him. I knew his secrets. I knew his heart. The world, at large, simply did not.

My father's two daughters were beautiful, like real can be beautiful, not like physicality can be beautiful. It was so much more than that. Leslie, also holding a glass of wine, was quietly taking in the casual scene. The lights were bright in the room. She was at the dining room bar area when she suddenly looked my way and smiled a knowing smile, called me over, hugged me. The wine always made her more easy.

"Now, don't think too much, Lizzy. I can see it in your eyes!" I smiled and acted like she was crazy. Of course she always saw everything in my face.

My father took my hand in his as Don Williams sang "Good Ole Boys Like Me." I felt myself float, never the dancer, but in my father's arms, he moved me effortlessly across the floor.

"Follow my lead, my sweet Lizzy Brat," he would always say, knowing I could never dance.

I was the odd child, the one with severe social anxiety. It was crippling, but he knew me better than I knew myself.

"Yes, Daddy," I would whisper in the sweetest voice that was somehow always reserved for only him. Many parts of me weren't really the person I was when I spoke to the most elegant man, my father. Don Williams sang and my daddy danced me.

The song filled my heart like magic. Don William's voice was pure magic. In the song there is a young man who's valuing the life he came from, a Southern life, and he's remembering it completely, even the smells.

The young man in the song sees his life, he knows how to look beneath the surface of it, and there seems to be a lamenting over belonging, but not belonging anymore. He talks about having to make a choice, learning to "talk like the man on the six o'clock news." I related to this song completely.

It's hard to be the person that looks over the top of your life, who observes it all, and you just know that you're going away from it, that it will only live in your memory.

"Why on earth this song, Lizzy?" he asked me seriously, but I didn't have an answer for him. I couldn't put into words that the song was an image trapped in time, and that was the very way that my brain worked. My brain trapped time.

The song made me feel my father, my siblings, my life before, and if I were to have an opportunity to dance with my father, I wanted a song that brought our highest truths to light, much in the way that this book is written.

Unfortunately, for my temporary husband, my life wasn't about the wedding or the unhappy marriage to come. My life was always about them, my siblings, my father and my mother. My entire existence was always tied up in what had brought my journey..., me..., to my knees, and made me not know how to live. I hope someday the man I married can forgive me that.

My father wanted Johnny Mathis. I gave him me. I spent so many hours in the front seat of his truck listening to Johnny Mathis, and I loved it.

"Don't touch the glass, Lizzy Brat." Sometimes in a daydream I would forget and touch the window glass. It was funny. He was sweet and meticulous about everything.

I hope whenever he hears the Don Williams song, forever, that he will remember me. Sometimes a song is all we have to give to someone.

My father never pushed me away, but I'm not in his life. I never knew how to be. That hurt never goes away. I feel like I failed us, the two of us, somehow.

I "learned to talk like the man on the six o'clock news." I never belonged anywhere with them all, ever again, if I ever did.

4

LESLIE

I saw her in a crowd recently. Her tall, bird-like features swayed with a certain gait that let me know that the person walking had had scoliosis. I hadn't seen her in years, but some things never change: her walk, her energy. I felt warm inside just knowing she and I were in the same world. I loved her. I would always remember her.

Leslie was wispy, beautiful, and unnervingly good all of our lives. I'd watched her be there for so many people through the years. She would give her last dollar to anyone who may have needed it. She was the bartender who lightened every room and every conversation; she was much like our father in that way. Leslie was a classy lady.

I was mesmerized by her charisma when I was a teenager. I'd asked her how it was that the whole world gravitated toward her, no matter where we were. She teasingly would say, "You're the only woman in the room, Lizzy. Young or old, when you walk into the room, just know you're the only woman there. Never doubt yourself, confidence is everything." I laughed with her, but I also contemplated her thoughts for most of my life.

"Gee, Lizzy, you'd be so beautiful if you'd just let go a little bit." She laughs. "You think too fucking much!" Leslie had such pretty blonde hair and her smile was larger than life.

A woman has to be confident, she said. A woman has to be sure, and no matter what happens in life, you're the only woman in the room. "Always have a smile on your face, Lizzy!"

This was Leslie's advice to me, but it meant so much more. Leslie never took herself too seriously, and that's what she was teaching me. Just lighten up! Make life a game! Be happy!

My sister skipped the bad stuff in human relationships. She had girlfriends in large numbers, she laughed with them, and she laughed at herself. She was simply undaunted. She always had the boyfriend on her arm. And for the record, in the privacy of home, she did not think of herself as a beautiful woman. She always teased about how she would go get some breasts one day. She was tiny all over. She would laugh and strut around the room jutting out her tiny bosom and tiny bottom. I thought she was lovely!

At fifteen I'd had a hard time with cleanliness, from what I now understand to be my OCD. I dealt in small ways with Obsessive Compulsive Disorder. I had this problem that if my panties fell on the floor or touched anything, I had to rewash them. When Leslie realized that, she was just excited to no end. She yanked my pink panties out of the pile of laundry on my bed, and stood dangling them between two fingers into the air in front of me.

"Look what I got, Lizzy!!" She flashed this hysterical and devious grin. She had one hand on her hip and one leg cocked sideways. I'll never forget it.

"What are you doing? Give those back!" I laughed back at her.

"No, I think I'm gonna drop them on the floor." She eyed me hysterically, like, watcha gonna do about it? You can't stop me now. "No, maybe I'll just touch everything in the room with them."

She started dancing around the room, touching the dresser, walls, light switch, and so on, with my pink panties in hand. I just laughed out loud. I already knew I'd have to rewash the panties.

She darted around the room in short shorts and a t-shirt, bird-like as always. "Could you give me my panties back, please?" I asked between spurts of laughter.

She paused with a deepened smile, "No, I don't think I will." She swirled the panties into the air like a helicopter propeller. "What if I just accidentally dropped your panties right here, would that bother you…, huh…, Lizzy?"

"No, as a matter of fact, I don't care," I couldn't stop laughing.

She held the panties still, into the air, and made a face like she was terribly serious. She dropped the panties, as I hysterically yelled, "NO," in this long pealing plea.

We both were looking as the panties hit the floor, but Leslie said, "Now, Lizzy," still serious, trying not to laugh, "Watch this!" She then jumped like a four year old, with both feet together, slipping and sliding with jumps, up and down on my panties, working them into the carpet, while laughing out of control. I was laughing out of control too. She looked crazy, staring at me, laughing wickedly at first, like, "Ha ha, look what I've done," but then losing it.

There were many times after that that she dangled my panties into the air in front of me, or did some other silly thing to make me laugh. That's what life was like with Leslie.

I love you, Leslie. Goodbye.

5

GOODBYE, MOTHER

Susan was the only mother of my life. Susan tipped the balance of what I would do with my time here. Isn't that the person who's truly your mother? The one person that made you look at your life so hard that you wanted to blackout, or the one person that made you look at your life so hard that you made something beautiful out of it? For better or worse, Susan was my mother. It's what I believe, and that's what matters, in an individual life.

Kay was a bystander of memory, a cause of a family's history, and a product, like we all were, of the greater destiny. Kay brought me to the planet, and I mean no disrespect in saying that that was all she had done for me.

One time, when I was a little girl, I was riding in the car with Susan when she reached out and touched me on my leg, ever so gently. I looked up at her in surprise. I'd not had her ever touch me like that, and she gave me the largest, warmest smile. I smiled back, as natural as could be. I wanted her to love me. It was the only time I'd ever known her touch to be gentle. I was seven years old at the time, before Al came into our lives.

Susan loved the music of Percy Sledge. His songs marked the rise and fall of her feelings. When I would come home from school to find her stereo blasting, as it did on the rare occasions when she was happy, she would be spending time with Percy Sledge, staying in her own head, and leaving me alone.

When my mother was happy, or in her own head, I felt free, like I felt when a heavy rain would come. Whenever it would rain, a separate self of myself would step out into it, holding her little hands out, greeting the rain, pausing the pain of living, for a time. I felt washed clean.

When the music was on, I could relax into the wild, soulful difference in the energy around me. When my mother listened to Percy Sledge, I took it as the times when she was still dreaming of a life, of possibility. A boyfriend or a husband usually followed. I do not begrudge her trying to wish herself a life. I would never have taken away her choices. We're all just muddling through our human experience.

I listen to Percy Sledge now because my mother taught me to love the music. Like so many abused children, I'd inadvertently learned to honor all the sides of a bizarre parent, not with approval, but with private vigil. Mother taught me to live in the gray, where there was no wrong or right.

My favorite song will always be Percy Sledge's "The Dark End of the Street." To me, the song summed up my feelings, at an early stage of the journey. I was taught by my mother that life for some only happens at the dark end of the street, "hiding in shadows where we don't belong."

I was the little girl at the dark end of the street. I hid in my mother's shadows, and in the shadows of a multiple personality disorder, until I was thirty-six years old. No one can ever look at me and say, "You're this, or you're that, or you've done this wrong thing!" It's not because they're wrong in accusing me, but because I won't believe them. I've walked through the world in shrouded gray, quite alone, and I believe I'm the only one that gets to decide who I am. It's my gift to myself, to honor me, to demand my own voice, in my life.

I sat in the oversized floral chair in my mother's living room when I was fifteen years old. My mother was taking a nap. I was talking on the phone to a boy that I really, really cared about. My young boyfriend was mad at me. I was pleading with my boyfriend to talk to me and to not hang up on me again, when at that moment I felt the lightness of my hand as the phone was gently raised from my possession.

My mother put the phone down in the receiver, looked me directly in the eyes, and said, "No daughter of mine will ever beg a man for anything. That's not the way it's done!" She turned and walked away without another word.

I'll always remember that time with the phone. My mother was right and I knew it. In a small way she had given something back to me. I sat there alone. She had forgotten me and headed into the kitchen, but she had freed me somehow.

The boy called me back, the phone was ringing wildly. I turned and walked down the long hall to my room. I felt free, and I loved my mother in that moment for giving me that strength.

Mother said that it wasn't done that way, and I was never again that pleading, desperate person. Mother made me even more careful about who I was, but in a better way, she inadvertently told me that I was valuable, that I should care about who I was, and not allow myself to be treated badly.

Over her last years, my mother asked me to come back home so many times that I can't remember them all. Sometimes I would visit and try to see her, but I had too many old things in my head to be able to cope with her house, to walk down the brown paneled hall to my little prison of a room ever again.

In a conversation we had, just before I told her about my multiplicity, long before her death, my mother asked me to come home. I think I broke her heart with my response.

"Lizzy, it's wrong that you stay away. I am your mother. I haven't seen you for so long. I don't believe I have much time left, Lizzy!" Her voice showed her tired age, and I recoiled at the "I haven't got much time left" part of the discussion.

"I'm sorry, I can't come right now. I'm working things out." I felt my own voice like it was a repetitive whisper to anyone that might care.

"Lizzy, I don't have much time left. Forget about the past!" She had a tinge of fear in her voice that I'd never detected before.

"No, I will not forget about the past! And…guess what… I'm not choosing to hold on to the past! The past holds on to me!" I felt angry, but still always careful when speaking to her, the enemy, the dark sky that hovered above my haunted forest. I'd often wondered if my soul would finally settle down if she would die.

"I don't know what you mean, Lizzy. I was a good mother! I did the best I could!" I felt her fear, and I heard my breath actually suck back into my lungs where I held it.

"NO YOU WEREN'T!" My voice crept up like ice. I'd never in my life, ever, stood up to that woman.

"What, what do you mean? I did the best I could raising you kids by myself!"

After the silent moment of disbelief, holding my breath again and letting go, I told her, "No you weren't a good mother. I'm sorry that things were so hard for you, and I do not blame you for anything. You had a hard life yourself, but....you can't lie to yourself like this any longer. You were not a good mother. You have to know it."

Her voice was choking, old and fearful.

"My counselor tells me I have to forgive myself for that! I've forgiven myself for that! I had to raise you kids by myself!" She wasn't identifying what "that" was, but we both knew what "that" was.

"Yes, ma'am, you're right, you must forgive yourself for "that." I really hope you can. I'd never have you leave the world carrying that kind of burden with you. I really wouldn't."

"You're not coming to see me, are you?" Her voice caused an ache inside of me that can never be forgotten. She did that to me. Mother brought so many things that couldn't be forgotten to my tired, prism-like, mind.

"No ma'am, I can't. I'm sorry."

"If it means anything, Lizzy, I'm sorry about all the things that I did. I am. I'm sorry." Her voice was defeated and lost.

My mother, Susan, taught me about the dark end of the street. All of life was a secret with her, and to her this was good. I don't know why. Secrets brought different things to our lives, like camaraderie in pain, a deepened love-hate connection with each other, and a self that's always trying to get out of self.

Mother was fond of saying, "In life, never let your left hand know what your right hand is doing." I pondered these words often in my childhood. Mother just meant "Play life close to your vest" with others, even those you think you trust.

For me, though, I was a dissociative child. I actually had parts of self that were split off from other parts of self. I lived childhood cutting off the pain, never looking back.

I would hum my mother's lesson, playing with Gretchen in the tub: "Don't let your right hand know what your left hand's doing," over and over again. It was all rather intricate and confusing. I had no one to trust or that I wanted to trust, except for my inner world where I lived when I had to escape. So I could only hide things from myself! I only had secrets from myself!

Gretchen watched me as I played. I'd put my left hand behind my back and move something into hiding with my right hand, and then I just knew in my brain that the left hand had lost the moved object forever. Then I'd switch, and do it with the other hand. In this simple way my mother reinforced that I learn to hide myself and what was happening to me, even from myself, for many, many years. Dissociative Identity Disorder made me a pro at hiding myself from myself, while mother reinforced my way of existing.

Mother decided and created the world.

I never thought I would survive her, but I did survive her, and I bring more context and meaning to a picture that she created. Mother was born a force and a whirlwind of soul. And I write, living my life, still in awe of her and her deliberate secrets. I'm still struggling to bring myself to the forefront of my own consciousness, not wanting to always "hide in shadows where I don't belong."

LIVING
IN THE
PRESENT

1

IMAGINE

Maybe my counselor would say, *"Imagine all of your parts of self in one room. Can you do that? Close your eyes now, concentrate. Can you bring all of your different parts of self to one room? She would say this in her kindest, softest voice.*

"I don't know," I could say then, ever so softly back, contemplating the idea.

"Come now," she would say. "Think of a place where all of your parts of self would feel safe and at the same time be face to face with each other."

I'd think deeply and say, "The ocean, we'd all feel safe at the ocean." I'd seem a little excited then.

"Wonderful," she would say. "Now, imagine all of your selves joining together on the beach maybe. Can you do that? Can you tell me what that would look like?"

My eyes would hurt a little from the squeezing. "We couldn't step on the beach together; we would have to have a safe room."

"Okay, okay, this is good. Tell me what the safe room looks like?"

"Well, I think it looks like a room on the wall of a cliff. It's jutting out over a stormy sea. The walls, except for the very back wall, are all glass. The sea is raging, just like our souls. We always feel like we're about to explode into something unexplainable."

"Good, good, you're doing so well. What else do you see in the picture? Is there a place for all of you to sit?"

"Oh yes," I'd say. "Yes, it looks like a conference room inside. Most of us are sitting at the table, but there are a few that don't understand that they're a part of our system. They look through the

others; they just don't see anyone else. No one minds really, it's just the way of things."

"Okay, we have a large table, glass walls over a stormy sea; can you tell me what the sounds are?"

"Sure, there is no sound, and we don't talk, of course. It's quite wonderful really. We can see the raging ocean on the other side of the glass, but we're in a soundproof room. We feel a glorious sense of belonging to the ocean, like we're immune to its wrath. We're not afraid and the ocean seems to be able to act out in a way that we can't."

"This is really good," she would say then. "Can you share more?"

"Well, my six year old self is sitting in one huge black office chair just jostling her seat back and forth. She's wearing her aqua blue clothes with the spotted dogs on them. The one of us that's in charge of the pictures just folds her arms in a womanly way and gently paces back and forth from the glass wall to the back of the room. There is one part of self that isolates herself in a cubicle set up in the back, it's very small, and we can see her over it. There are several selves sitting around the table with the six year old. The most fascinating to me, though, is the part of self that clings to the front glass wall." I would take a long pause then.

"Why is she the most fascinating to you?" She would have raised herself in her seat with interest..., maybe..., maybe not.

"She's fascinating because she has some kind of spiritual connection with the ocean that makes her unable to decipher if it would really stop her breath if she slipped beneath it. She's dressed in black, which is her general color of choice. She's thin, long dark hair; her palms are stuck to the glass to the point that there are sweaty spots on the glass where her palms have rested. She spends her time contemplating oblivion. She studies a lot of Eastern meditation and spiritual theories so that she can come to the conclusion that it's okay to go ahead and end her life."

She would sit back then, if she were sitting forward. "Are you saying she wants to kill herself?"

"Of course." I would say this naturally. It wouldn't be meant to be shocking.

Coolly, she would ask, "Why doesn't she do it? Why doesn't she just kill herself?"

I have this feeling that maybe my eyes would be the only ones closed at this point. I would squeeze them tighter. "She doesn't do it, because she can't. There are too many parts of self in conflict for that to be a possibility. Our six year old part of self is very fragile and obsessed with death to an unnatural degree."

I'd open my eyes then.

I'd thank Meredith, my counselor of almost a decade.

Meredith would sit across from me, looking at me in her way. It was a way that I'd learned to trust. I trusted her room, the office and the smells in it. I trusted the new paint job, (lime green trim), although it was hard for me to accept the change. I trusted the brilliantly green golf course that I would gaze out at while we talked through the shattered pieces of my mind.

I trusted the fireplace, where I felt so at home just sitting there with Meredith on lazy afternoons. I trusted the peace lily that always seemed to be reaching out to me as I sat in my rolling black chair.

I trusted the rise and fall of Meredith's voice in the small room. Her room was only slightly larger than the brown paneled room that I'd grown up in. As a child, I had known that, one day, when I was all grown up, there would be a Meredith and I wouldn't be alone in any room ever again. I don't know how I knew this but I did.

I will carry Meredith in my heart, and I will never be alone again, not in my mind, not in my pain. I just trusted Meredith, and that's the point, I think.

Meredith was always on my side. She had always been my greatest life advocate. Meredith knew what to do to save my life. She knew how to help me love myself, and see that I had worth in the journey. She was so many things for so many years … before she recently retired.

It's a painful thing, new beginnings, but I know it's for the best. It was time to stand on my own, and decide if I would make something of the journey.

Meredith was my friend, and she loved me when I could not love myself.

2

STARTING TO HEAL

I haven't said much about my years of therapy, not because it's a point of shame, but because it's still a very sensitive topic for me. I do understand, though, that my work with my counselor has its place in what I'm trying to explain. My going to counseling is a part of the truth that I'm telling, and it's a part of my journey.

When I finally told my counselor, Meredith, about the incident in the car with Al, we'd been working together for many years. She was glad that I could finally discuss something specific that would help with my inner dynamic. I was not forthcoming with my memories, and the fragments of my half-memories, for a great deal of the time. My different selves always made me stay more on the surface. I had a mediator self while working with Meredith, who regulated what could be talked about in the beginning, and what could not be talked about.

I discussed happenings in my life, dealing with a hard marriage, my mother, and issues with low self esteem for most of our early years together. And, of course, my sexual abuse, but only with the information that my parts of self would allow me to give, enough for us to talk about the topic. Meredith knew all along what I was doing and why, but I just could not accept, even though I knew that I was managing this elaborate system, that I had D.I.D., or multiple personalities. She told me within the first year that she was watching me change selves in front of her. My mediator self just wouldn't believe her; we could only accept that Meredith could see the mediator. We would not acknowledge openly what was happening in any way.

I think we didn't want to believe her, or accept the D.I.D. because my parts of self did not take over to the degree where I would lose great periods of time in adulthood. I did lose a lot of time in childhood.

It's those young selves that I deal with in my adult life today. I had experiences back then where I would wake up not knowing how many days I'd lost, but understanding that I had in fact lost them. Sometimes I would wake to a different day of the week than the one that it was supposed to be. Sometimes I'd wake up wearing clothes that I didn't remember putting on. Sometimes I'd wake up from sleeping in a place that I'd not remembered going to sleep in. I knew time had gone on without me a lot of the time as I grew older. I remember stumbling around my mother's house trying to find clues to where life was at, in that moment in time, because I'd come back and I had to get a hold on things again. Losing time made me feel unreal and like I could disappear forever and not even know it myself. To say that it was frightening could never really explain the kind of fear that time loss brings to a person.

Another reason that I didn't believe that I had true DID was that I had read Sybil when I was a teenager, and I thought you had to be like Sybil to have DID. I didn't know that you could have DID in different degrees.

In the end Meredith and I had a talk about my denial. She told me that she had to work on my self esteem, my current life, and build me up where she could, so that I would be strong enough to accept the DID. I can't think of what I ever would have done with my life had I not had Meredith in it, guiding my way.

It's possible that Meredith recognized my dissociation within the first months of our sessions. It's possible that she knew in the first five minutes. I am sorry that I fought the truth of what I am for a lot of my life. But, isn't that the way of things, paced out into what we gather up, in the end?

I lived in a world that I had created to protect myself, and somehow Meredith watched over me, and knew how to get into my very isolated and gated existence. I couldn't personally maneuver in my world, but she could.

Meredith is a deeply spiritual woman. I've always had an understanding, in some capacity, that the universe was putting tools in my path to help me on my way. Meredith was one of those tools. I couldn't have done the things in my life that I have done if it weren't for Meredith carrying me through.

One day I was talking about being in the car, that day with Al with the red water pump, the day the worst of it all began.

"What could you tell yourself in the car, that day with Al, to ease some of the fear that you were feeling?" Meredith sat across from me in the kind of green colored shirt my mother used to wear. Seeing her in it made me feel world-weary.

"I couldn't say anything." I'd drug myself in to see Meredith, still in pajamas that day.

"Come on now, try. What could you tell yourself in the car if you could go back in time and make things better?"

"Nothing," I said flatly. I was staring out the French doors that overlooked the greenest golf course. I felt pain and pressure in my mouth from my involuntary tightening of my jaw off and on.

"Maybe you could tell yourself that things will be okay? Just try to imagine what you could say to help with the pain."

"I don't want to think about her, I don't want to imagine her. I'm never going back in time to her." The truth of my disconnection came out again. I had to call myself, "her."

"It could help you, though, to go back in time to yourself and let yourself know that things would be okay later," she suggested.

"What do you want me to say to *her*?" I felt mad, or caught in something I didn't want to be in.

"I can't tell you what to say. You have to decide." I laughed out loud when she said this. I felt like, wow, what a ridiculous journey to be having. What a trap!

I felt really loud then, half between laughter and madness. "You know what I think; I think I don't even like her. I think I feel the same way about her that those church gossips did. I think she's carried a sign on her forehead her entire life that said she was "that kind of girl." I think she came into the world, one of those kinds of kids. I think she's pathetic. I don't like her."

Meredith nodded her head, and I could see that she felt bad that I thought about my life, my selves, in the way that I did. "I think you're right about that. I think you believe all the bad things that others have told you about yourself."

Suddenly, I felt the truth of my use of "her" in a way that I didn't before. I was listening to myself practically blame some unknown girl, who actually was me, about the life she lived. It became clear that I wasn't owning my life, or myself. I did not want to think of myself as the person who was in the car with Al.

Every once in a while, in the early days with Meredith, I tried to find some other problem that wasn't Dissociation to explain my behaviors to myself, but when it was slammed in front of me, because I always said "her" when referring to my past, like I wasn't talking about me, I was pushed deeply into my dissociative reality.

The room was quiet. "Liz, just work on something you might say, before I see you again. Do you think you could do that?"

"I don't know," I sat staring at her. "I always feel better when I leave here. I feel confused about leaving with something I can't resolve." I was sad, and used to leaving her office in a pumped up and solid state.

"This time is just going to require a little more adjustment and working through your thinking about it. Think of your own daughter. What would you tell your daughter if she were the person in that situation?"

"I hate it when you do that! My daughter isn't me; she is different and her life has been guarded by me!"

"What made you different from her? You just didn't have anyone taking care of you."

"Rationally, I get what you're saying. I know kids don't come into the world marked, but right now it just doesn't feel that way to me, not when we talk about the car and that day. It alters my perceptions, my feelings."

"What if I brought in a line of children? Would some children act in a way that invites sexual abuse and others not?" Meredith was talking slowly, leaning forward in the terrible silky green shirt. I knew she was mixing up my thinking about things; she was good at that. She knew how to make the picture look different, which sometimes helped me out of my world.

"I don't want to think about children. I don't like children anymore." I started playing with a leaf on the peace lily that over the years had become my friend.

"Come on now, what if I brought in a line of random children? Do some of them just scream out, "Abuse me, please?" She had her hands in the air for dramatic effect.

"I don't like small children anymore. I like my daughter, my son.

I like my two little cousins. I can control my feelings about them, but I don't want to be around other children anymore. I especially can't stand to see mistreated children anymore. I used to want to make a difference with children, but now I just want their eyes to never look into my eyes. I feel haunted. Children make me uncomfortable. I don't feel like myself anymore when I'm around children."

"I understand, but you're not answering." Meredith was patient.

"I can't answer today."

"Okay, just think about it until I see you again."

I laughed and looked into her eyes. I couldn't have been more defeated. "I need a mystic to show my life to me, to unfold it in front of me, to give it an understandable meaning and philosophical ease."

Meredith smiled at me. I guess I was really saying that I needed someone stronger than myself to make sense of the things that happened in my journey, because I wasn't really strong enough to do the job that only I could do. Meredith held my life up, but she couldn't bring memories from my mind, and she couldn't force my different selves to talk if I didn't let them. I had to give her something to work with.

We parted for that day's session. I was very dismayed. I really had always felt better after I left Meredith's office. Only a few times had we discussed things that I couldn't make peace with.

A miraculous thing happened, though, when I got into my car, or at least it was miraculous to me, in my mind. I'd been listening to my Carolyn Myss audio of her Energy Anatomy. I'd gotten it years before, and decided to revisit it. The first line I'd heard when I started the car was something about a mystic, which brightened my heart. I felt peace. I don't even remember exactly what she said. I just knew she was saying something about a mystic and I was just in Meredith's office talking about how I needed one.

I kept listening to Myss that afternoon; she, over time, has taught me a great many things. On this day, though, something she taught sank in that didn't quite sink in with me before, and it was that my family *wasn't* supposed to love me in a way that made me stay with them forever in my life's journey. They were supposed to love me in a way that *pushed* me from the nest. I suddenly understood that my family was sending me off to do different things in my life, in the world, things that I couldn't have done had I not known them or been a part of their family, things that I could not have done had I stayed among them. I had to know them, my family, but then I had to learn that I didn't belong with them for all of my life. Nothing was personal; what they had done to me was all just a part of a greater picture.

My family was supposed to love me in a way that made me evolve in the ways that I would need to evolve to live a different sort of life than the one I was born to. This teaching finally sinking in was a heavy load off of me. It was finally okay for me, what my family had been in my life. Somehow it made me finally feel like it was me, myself, me, sitting in the car with Al.

I called Meredith, and left her a message, that I knew what to say to myself in the car with Al.

I would say to that little girl, "Twenty years from now, you're going to meet a counselor, or lady, who's going to be able to help you in your life. This nice and beautiful lady will spend ten years with you, helping you feel good, like regular people get to feel good, who really get to live a real life. In twenty years, you won't be afraid of living so much anymore, because this lady will take care of you and teach you how to take care of yourself. She will really see you, she will really love you, and she's going to really believe in her heart that you're something special. Mostly, though, you just won't be alone anymore because of her." I'd tell the little girl in the car to just hold on until the day you find a woman named Meredith.

I don't really know what else to say, about the car, about Al, or the red water pump. I just know now that what I lived, and the growth and development that I've had, has made me something better in the bigger picture of my life.

I do have to say, though, that I'm sorry to that younger part of self who was me. I'm sorry, little Lizzy, that I thought you were something ugly or bad. You were stronger than I ever was to be able to keep such control in your terrible experiences. Thank you for sharing your experiences with Al in this record. Your voice was still and mature. Your way of looking at the world was regulated and true. You might be the most beautiful one of us in your steadfast and dreamy nature.

3

THE SEASONAL SOUL

I wrote when I was young about a fear I'd had in my heart of finding that my soul was somehow seasonal. I didn't mean the seasons of the year. Writing about the seasons was a metaphor for what was happening to me inside. I wrote then, "I miss my mother, I miss my father, but most of all, I miss myself, and I'm afraid to know that my soul is seasonal."

In this seasonal metaphor, and in my childlike way, I meant to explain that I noticed about myself that my feelings of safety inside of myself changed instantly with sudden unique smells, with odd noises, and with some weather conditions that coincided with an odd light at a certain time of day. I felt scared all of the time in childhood, just by living. I was never a stable self. I didn't adapt well when I came into my human experience here, in this time.

I described my soul as seasonal then, but in essence, I think I must have understood on some level that I had many triggers that my psyche would respond to that were out of my control, and those triggers would change me into another part of self. In my childlike way I was openly saying that I wasn't coping with the journey. I was always in a constant state of change, a shape shifter that no one could really see, or so it felt to me, in my child's mind.

I believed in early life that I was mentally ill, and acted in a way to conceal that fact. It didn't help that my mother was always threatening to put me in an insane asylum from the age of seven, for no apparent reason other than to bring me pain.

Even though I hid who I was from Mother, I didn't have control over my depressions, my anxiety with others, or a sick feeling that sometimes turned my stomach instantly, out of the blue. I held onto sanity, though, with all of my conscious might, a sanity that seemed to constantly elude me.

I just didn't know, when I was young, how to cope inside of myself with all of the pain that I carried. All I knew was loss, lost time mostly, lost pictures to take in my mind, and the loss of being trapped without love in a mental disorder.

Sometimes people would ask me, people who knew my family while I was growing up, how I lived through all of the things my mother did to me. They would have this look of knowing something about me that they could not have known. I didn't know what they wanted from me. I felt paranoid, and specifically private. I would look them in the eye, waiting for their summary, being utterly confused by anyone's audacity to call out my life. I felt defensive when they asked me how I survived my mother.

The person asking would be living some life I wouldn't understand and looking at me with such pity, like the church gossips. It's hard to face the people who are voyeurs of our pain. I would just leave the room, change the subject, just move on somehow, from that kind of person.

I've walked through my adult life confessing to an anxiety disorder that I do not have, and this seems to have gotten me by when people have noticed the oddness, the obscurity, of me. I've never liked confessing something that wasn't true, in trying to maneuver life. I'd rather be who I am.

I'm an integrating dissociative person. I have a handful of alters left in my integration process. I've learned to love all of my selves, to have compassion, and to know the truth of my life. I'm proud of this.

I've never been unpredictable. I've lived a very isolated life, but my demeanor has spun in many different directions in social settings. People have talked to my different parts of self and they never noticed that I wasn't integrated; their confusion comes when they meet me again and I act in a completely different way than I had before. Anxiety is the word I use to explain any odd behavior that comes forth. People leave you alone then; they let you go.

I've appeared odd in life, at different times, and for the most part I've known it. It doesn't hurt me anymore to be so different, and I don't know that it really hurt. I guess I can say it's been exhausting, and it's less exhausting for me now. I've stopped pretending that I'm one part of self in front of the world. I let my selves live. We are integrating, and cooperating in that process.

I feel happy in that admission. I've gone through stages of not wanting to believe that I was a multiple. I'd talk with my counselor about other possibilities, while she would put her head in her hand and gaze at me for a period of time. It's our funniest of sessions, but maybe not. She sits with her sweetest but firmest expressions, rocking in her chair. Then I'll sputter, "Forget it, it's fine, my other parts of self don't like it anyway when I try to pretend other solutions for my kaleidoscope mind." Then my counselor and I move on to whatever's on the agenda for the day.

It used to seem like I was at the bottom of a well when I first understood what was wrong with me. At first I was frightened that I'd never have a fully integrated life, but then, in time, I understood that this was my journey. For whatever reason, it's what I'm doing with my time here.

As a multiple, sometimes I'm exhausted by existence. Social situations are the worst. People's behaviors, smells, and energies trigger unforeseen reactions, and I get confused about how to act in different situations. I try to act like the part of self that came to the dinner party as an adult, while someone's cologne is making my younger part of self want to find a dark corner to sit in and clutch herself. I get headaches whenever I switch, but I have always hidden my multiplicity, always. I've never actually taken myself into a quiet corner and started clutching myself in ranting tears. Not that there's anything wrong with that.

Some of my younger parts of self don't have a mother. They don't claim Susan or Kay. They lack commitment to any decision as to who their mother really is. They nod it off. There's no conclusion. We're working on that! This is where my phrase, "the Mother," comes from.

I'd like to thank whatever higher form that's looked out for me my entire life. I felt it there in the brown paneled closet, with the green rough carpet under my bare bottom. I felt it there like I would feel eyes on me in the densest crowd.

I've never been able to believe in any physical reality. It's been too concretely temporary, me with my translucent fingers and me with my precarious mind. The seasons change and I breathe deeply. It's all going by so quickly. I know, in my heart, that I am Spirit.

When I started out with this record of my life, I thought I was writing this account of my and my siblings' lives to save us all from invisibility, but I've since learned that I was the only one in my family that was ever invisible.

And, I was only invisible to myself. It appears now that I write this record for my mother, not the ones that I thought I was writing it for.

She was not puritanical in nature, my mother. She did not live a moral life. My mother was many different parts of a whole, and I don't want to lose the fact that I did love the parts of her that exhibited so much strength. No, I am not implying that my mother was a multiple like myself. I'm saying that she had many aspects to her, and some of them mattered in my life.

I forgive my mother, for her negligence, and for her carelessness with my life. I forgive her for the world, and I hope that she can forgive me. I didn't judge her, but she felt judged, and I'm so sorry about that. She was my mother.

When the people you need to love you can't love you, you learn to seek a greater experience.

So, thank you, Mother, for making me who I am today. Thank you, Mother, for helping me become a multiple, so that I would have to learn to know myself. Thank you, Mother, for the things that I don't know yet, that will come to light, in the journey, that my dissociation will help me with. Thank you for the alliance, Mother, of being a woman so similar to you, but so different from you at the same time.

It was no mistake that you became my mother. It was written, I think, well before our time. I'm not ashamed of you. I'm proud of your efforts in life, and I hope you will always be proud of me. What a woman you were! What a powerful and beautiful life we shared! It was life, and it was great, what we had with each other.

4

TELLING MOTHER

ABOUT MY MULTIPLICITY

W hen I walked into my mother's house the last time, that night not so long ago, she was surprised. She looked up, momentarily stunned, but then lit a cigarette. What was it about people and cigarettes in those days? Her face had changed, altered from the mother I'd envisioned that I would see, because it had always been her face. Age and poor health had made my mother look like a different person, and it was my first time having the experience of seeing a person's physical form lost.

I longed for the mother of strength that I'd always known. Where had her face gone? Where was her olive coloring? Her eyes were small; the lights were out. Her movements, even to smoke, seemed to be draining for her.

Did she know what I saw when I looked at her? Was she aware that she was gone, forever? I was heartbroken, taken aback, and why on earth did it always matter anyway? It might have been that there was an invisible clock ticking, and I knew that I was running out of time to ever make my peace with her.

It was all too much for me.

"I wanted to tell you that I don't have bad feelings about you. That I understand that you lived a very hard life." We were sitting at her kitchen bar.

"I don't want to think about the past anymore," she replied, giving me the noncommittal, exhausted wave of her hand, trying to erase my reality.

"I know, I know. I'm sorry about that," I apologized, sorry to cause her pain.

She puffed away on her cigarette, asked me to bring her a glass of ice water. I felt happy that some things didn't change. "Make sure you wash your hands before you get the ice."

"Yes, ma'am. I came by because I wanted to tell you that I've been seeing a counselor for years and she's really helping me. I wanted to tell you that I don't stay away to be cruel, or anything like that, to you." I waited.

"Well, it's good that you have a counselor, I had a psychiatrist for years. They helped me a lot with the nightmares I couldn't stop having. They put me on medicine, though." She stared feebly away from me, at the mayonnaise jar, that, as usual, had stayed out way too long, lid off and all.

"I have something called Dissociative Identity Disorder." She steadily avoided my eyes. She appeared nervous. I wasn't sure in that moment if she knew what I was talking about.

"I have what people used to call Multiple Personality Disorder." Her face was animated with sudden horror. She straightened her back, grabbed her arms, seemed to wish I'd never come, and started to tremble. I saw it all, and I felt horrible that I'd told her, because I could see the blame of what she felt was a horror that she was attributing to herself.

"I'm okay; it's not as bad as you might think," I squeaked. "I'm not a severe case. I don't black out and lose time now…, but I did when I was little. Mostly what happens is that I have triggers that make me feel and act differently. It feels like I'm watching my behaviors from around myself. I have trouble getting to an adult core place, again."

"You're getting help. That's good." Mother was gone then, wishing she was in the living room watching Murder She Wrote, her favorite show late in her life.

"I've been integrating for some years, Mother. I don't want you to blame yourself."

"I don't blame myself. I did the best I could."

I studied her distant, different face, and felt alone like I always did. "Yes ma'am, you did. Well, I'd appreciate it if you didn't tell anyone. It's not a very bad case anyway. I don't struggle so much with my different forces as others in my situation do. I don't have other names, Mother."

I said this like it was ever going to make any difference. My alters don't have specific names; they live within their different natures, which is the same thing. I have clear and separate identities; some have been clearer defined selves than others.

"Mother, are you hearing me?" She looked frightened, taken aback still.

Knowing she was an avid reader I said, "Mother, it's not like Sybil's case. It's not that complicated for me, but it's my understanding that Sybil integrated and did great things with her life." My mother still sat, eyes frozen on the mayonnaise jar.

"Mother, people make dissociation a scary thing, it's not! We all dissociate to some degree. My removing my mind in trauma simply got a little more complicated. I separated from myself."

I suddenly felt desperate. I couldn't dare go into explaining to her that this is what children do to survive serious trauma. I'd clearly put her into what she felt was a twilight zone, and I didn't know how to make it better for her. I felt mortified and ashamed of what I had done. It just never occurred to me, with her being a reader, and always being in control of everything, that I could have knocked her off balance. It was bad, and I felt bad!

"I'll never tell anyone," she muttered.

I gathered my things to go. "Thank you for not telling anyone."

She didn't say anything else.

She'd lost her ability to dial the world and make every experience her own. This, I was, of course, glad of. I was sad, though, for the reasons I knew that this time my mother would keep my secret: It wasn't because she would finally do what was right for me. It was because she was afraid of me and she felt that she created my disorder. It was sad all the way around.

I guess it's good that my mother appeared to be somebody else that day and wore a different face, because the mother I'd always known would've been brave enough to hear me. I couldn't have borne my reality in those moments, if my mother had not been masked.

5

BREAKING THE CYCLE

When my daughter was very little, maybe two, I took her by to visit my mother. It was when my mother was still somewhat present. I remember sitting at the bar with my mother. My mother was smoking and drinking coffee. My daughter was mad at me for not allowing her to have something that she wanted. My daughter threw herself down, tantrum style, on the floor.

With my mother and me at the bar, my daughter was lying flat on her back, kicking and screaming, trying to have her way. I ignored my daughter's outburst that day, but a lot of times I gave in. I was never a very strong disciplinarian. My mother looked from my daughter and back to me, in utter disbelief, over and over again.

"Are you going to let her do that?" she asked. Her eyes were wide with amazement.

"Yes, yes, I am!" I looked at my mother. I was feeling this reality: my mother never let us breathe in her presence, but she was watching her own daughter's daughter act in a way that was completely alien to her thoughts.

"You're going to let her lie there and scream her natural head off!?"

"Yes, yes I am." I felt a smile inside of myself. I might have been glowing. My voice was as natural and sweet as anything.

"She's stronger than you, Lizzy. Do you know that?"

"Yes, ma'am, I know that." I was glowing; she'd just said everything I'd ever wanted to hear.

"You don't feel you need to stop her, control her?" My mother eyed me wildly.

"No, no I don't." I understood everything my mother was thinking.

"Lizzy, if you don't get a hold of that child now, you're headed for trouble down the road."

"Yes, ma'am, I understand." I flatly wouldn't engage in this kind of conversation with my mother.

My mother brutalized us. She beat some of us into submission, some of us into rebellion, and some of us into silence and drugs.

With my children, I didn't know the right way to discipline them. I had no model, but whatever way I did it, it would start with love. And what my mother didn't understand was that I had my own special issues to deal with in raising a daughter.

I would not allow my own daughter to take the abuse that I'd taken in my life.

I didn't want my daughter to be wild or out of control, but I did want her to have the strength of mind to be a woman who would stand up for her life, and fight for all that she believed in.

I did not want my daughter to have any fear, or any limits when it came to owning herself. It's true, I could have been a stronger disciplinarian. I treaded water slowly, trying to learn to give proper boundaries, while at the same time letting my daughter discover exactly who she was meant to be in the journey.

I must have done something right, by loving her, talking to her, being with her, because that defiant little girl is turning into the kindest and strongest person that I ever could have imagined in my life. I'm in awe of her and her brother, every day. It's been an honor to love them.

GOING HOME

AGAIN

I wasn't there when my mother's ashes were tossed high into the air. And my siblings didn't choose to spread her ashes on the river that she grew up on. They chose a different spot. I thought that was kind.

I wasn't there to see my sister dressed in black, or Jessie tall and unconquerable; I wasn't there to see how Quentin would look at me. That part, I made up.

Nothing else in this record is made up. This was my true life, as a child. With Jessie, I didn't know how to explain that he always caught my odd behaviors, so I used the part about the boat names, and his finding me in the dancing moonlight to explain it, but neither situation is very clear to me. Jessie found me doing odd things throughout childhood. The point is that Jessie knew something was wrong with me, before I did. He just never told anyone, or maybe he just didn't know what to make of my oddness.

In case I've said anything inaccurate about Al's life, I want to make it clear that I've never looked up his personal record or life history. My information comes from family discussions about his being in prison once or twice before he married my mother, and after he was married to my mother, because of the incident with Mrs. Edna's granddaughter. I heard through grownups that the granddaughter told her mother what Al was trying to do with her, and the little girl's mother put a stop to it. My understanding is that Mrs. Edna visited Al regularly during his new prison term. My understanding is that she refused to believe that Al would ever sexually abuse little girls.

I hope that Leslie can forgive the way that I've written the two of us together in the beginning of this record. The conversations I've written are not exact, but they are accumulative pieces of conversations, and hostilities that we've dealt with over the years.

I hope Brent can forgive me too, for ever mentioning the sexual history that we had. If I was seven or eight, maybe that would have made him thirteen or fourteen. Like I said before, I believe that he was probably abused as well. I think he was taught his behavior toward me, and it's a behavior that he never pressed upon me again after early childhood. We were all severely abused back then. I only revealed this aspect of the story because it was important to explain what I was living through at this particular time in my life.

Also, concerning Brent's drug and alcohol abuse, I knew that he drank and all the other parts that I explained in his section of the memoir, but I never saw the drugs personally. The drugs were what I understood from listening to grownup discussions about my brother.

I wasn't there when Mother's ashes were scattered. My siblings may have tried to let me know when this ceremony would take place, but I didn't answer my phone anyway, at the time, for fear of facing my life.

In the summer of 2007, right before she died, I drove out to my mother's house late in the night. I parked across the street from the house that I grew up in. I was parked on the bit of ground in front of Mr. Revel's house. I stared through the heavy trees at the light in her bedroom window, where she slept my whole life, where I knew she was reading novel after novel, that's what she always did, and it comforted me. I fought the urge to pass through the gate in the night, to walk up the concrete steps, to walk down the brown paneled hall, past my little room, to her room at the end of the hall.

I wanted her to comfort me. I wanted to be near her. She hadn't struck me, hit me, for many, many years. I wanted to bury my face in her blue green silky nightgown and have her be with me. I missed her violently, and I didn't know why.

Two weeks after parking across the street from my mother's house and not going in, I had a call from one of my mother's friends. I picked up my phone to see the number.

I'd oddly been waiting for that call. I felt it was coming. I waited for a message to be left: "Lizzy, don't tell anyone I called, but your mother's in the hospital. I think she's not coming out this time. I just wanted you to know."

I felt my face glow with heated shame since I didn't know what to do. I knew I would do nothing. I felt trembly, unstable even, but I put my mind on something else. I knew that my mother had asked everybody not to call me, but she still had probably had her friend call me secretly because she actually wanted to see me. I did nothing. I just packed a bag and left town, so that I would look like I was away when it happened. I just had a feeling.

When the call came that my mother had passed away, I didn't know what to think. I just felt my child-like inner world tighten.

Some part of myself, that didn't claim Susan as her mother, was very respectful about what this must have meant to our core. This part of self contemplated the profound news, deeply, like this part of me would do if she were a visiting relative from the country, and not quite part of our family.

Some other young part of self thought about how the Mother rubbed her leg once, and how she'd never have that again. I guess she was always waiting to be touched again with love by the Mother.

Some older part of self just felt like, "Damn, I thought I'd feel some kind of release when she passed, but Damn, it just makes me madder. WHY am I madder? I want to scream! What has she done to me by up and dying on me?"

Some younger part of self just felt loyalty to the Mother, and decided that she wouldn't lose the panoramic pictures. She doesn't understand that letting go of the pictures of our past doesn't mean that she herself will die.

All of these scenes must play over and over again in my mind, so, what do I do with that? What do you feel, when the world has taught you not to feel, and you're left stunned with the unresolved information?

When I heard that my mother was dead, my whole inner world drew up. I dropped the phone. I wanted to come out of my skin, but I couldn't. That's the one place where the line is drawn, even if you're a dissociative person.

Mother had gone home from the hospital, I'm not sure for how many days. Time gets blurry when I think about her death. She died peacefully in her sleep, or this is at least what I've been told. I'm glad that she passed away in her safe place, and in my heart I hope she didn't know what was happening.

I'd hate to think that she went alone, or afraid.

I haven't seen or heard from my siblings since before our mother died, and that's okay.

Someone asked me recently if I had any siblings, and this question, no matter how normal, will always catch me off guard. I find my inner world trying to decide if we do or do not have siblings, but of course, in concrete reality, we do. Everything really, in early life, is a point of contemplation for my elaborate system.

I miss Leslie, Quentin, Jessie, Brent, and Keith. Sometimes, I sit in my windowed hideaway, watching the trees swaying in the wind, and just think about them. It makes me feel good to think about my siblings, and that I was once a part of something different than the life I live today.

I can't explain it really, but it's like I've lived many lives in one, and I'm acknowledging that. Leslie used to say, "Lizzy, you think too much! Stop thinking and just live," and she would laugh because she loved me.

I miss them all.

I know that now my siblings are living life in a way that makes sense to them, and I'm happy for them, if they are happy. I think of my siblings as a unit, even with Brent, and I accept that I'm not in that unit anymore.

I did not accept that before. I just kicked and screamed internally, not knowing how to look at things without an aching inside that had no reprieve. I wanted so badly to belong, but I didn't. It's nobody's fault, and now I understand that my family was just a starting place for my journey. I accept that.

Though I feel alone, I'm not alone, but we're all alone, and that's the way that it is.

I can't go home again, in this life, and my siblings refuse to leave home. This leaves my mind, where they're concerned, in an introspective place, where I can quietly watch the scenes and contemplate the life that's gone by me. I'm in my self-made institution. I don't think my siblings want to see the patients in my world. I can forgive them that.

AFTERWORD

Are you clapping, Andrew? Did I hear the encore as the curtain fell? Were you in the wings just silently smiling? The stage was set with the colors of winter across a dark burnished wood. It was set with my tears and yours. I see your hands moving in slow motion like a promise after death. I see the soft compelling lines set in your face. I hear your sweet comic laughter like I held you just today. I see your body in weighty contrast to other men. You were tall, large, just different.

I see your clumsy stagger and the luring weight in your eyes. You stand there with approval, or with the only approval that I'd ever needed.

I'm entering the stage now from the audience's perspective. I'm climbing those large wooden stairs. There are no rails for me to hold on to. I've always been in wonderment over there being no rails to hold on to. I'm dressed in all black, a turtleneck, even. I walk across the bare wooden planks with my hands clasped together at my mouth. I didn't know what else to do, Andrew. Should I hang my hands and my head the way I did as a child, or must I hold my head up high as the tears come streaming down my face?

It's dark here, no spotlights, just a soft glowing haze. I slowly circle around from the center of the stage. I step forward to an audience of a few hundred empty chairs. It was a play, was it not? It was a play, but I tell you with all that I am that it was me. I've always been the play. I've always lived the invention. It was my role…, in my time…, it was me.

My hands clasped tightly together, I love the darkness, and I'm thankful to be alone to share this last moment with you. Your energy surrounds me the same way your body once did. I hear your clumsy walk. I turn and face what I believe is the essence of you. A haze surrounds the spirit of you in my mind. I hear the raspiness of your voice echo in the auditorium.

You're telling me, "Well, honey, couldn't it have been a happier ending?" I smile to myself and then to you as my hands fall for the first time, because that is, of course, exactly what you would say.

The image dies out slowly and the haze stays consistent. I never noticed the backdrop in its dark color variations. I spin around slowly, and the chairs are empty still. This is our moment, and I'm taking it in. My hands swing around me. I'm so small and insignificant on the stage with its clanking wooden planks. My smile broadens as I slowly make my way to the darkly tarnished switch on the wall.

You've left, and so now I am leaving. I never had a choice really. I feel my breath catch as I hit the switch and the light haze goes out.

www.ingramcontent.com/pod-product-compliance
Lightning Source LLC
Chambersburg PA
CBHW031248090426
42742CB00007B/355